HOW TO USE THIS SUPPLEMENT

The Second Supplement to the Thirteenth Edition of *Charlesworth & Percy on Negligence* is ordered according to the structure of the Main Volume.

At the beginning of the supplementary coverage for each Chapter the mini Table of Contents from the Main Volume has been included. Where a heading on this Table of Contents has been marked with a black square pointer then there is relevant information in the Supplement to which you should refer. A white square pointer indicates material that has been included from the previous Supplement.

Within each Chapter updating information is referenced to the relevant paragraph in the Main Volume. The instructions in the square brackets explain how the added material relates to the Main Volume.

TABLE OF CASES

TABLE OF STATUTES

TABLE OF STATUTORY INSTRUMENTS

TABLE OF CIVIL PROCEDURE RULES

TABLE OF EUROPEAN AND INTERNATIONAL CONVENTIONS

TABLE OF EUROPEAN DIRECTIVES

THE MEANING OF NEGLIGENCE

2.—NEGLIGENCE AS CARELESS CONDUCT

Negligence and "accident"

[Add to line 3 of n.17]   **1–10**

. . . suffered serious injury] also *Dunnage v Randall* [2016] P.I.Q.R. P1, CA (a similarly-worded insurance policy covered injuries suffered by the claimant when he attempted to prevent his uncle, who was suffering paranoid schizophrenia, setting fire to himself: the uncle's actions were not wilful or malicious because he had lost control of his ability to make choices and could not be said to have intended to injure the appellant, but objectively the uncle was in breach of his duty of care to the claimant and what happened was correctly characterised as an accident). [For the meaning . . .

3.—NEGLIGENCE AS THE BREACH OF A DUTY TO TAKE CARE

The third meaning

[Add new footnote reference 42a to "objectively" in line 2]   **1–19**

NOTE 42a. See *Dunnage v Randall* [2016] P.I.Q.R. P1, CA, para.1-10, n.17, above (the disturbed mental state of someone who attempted to set fire to himself did not prevent his owing a duty of care towards another person who attempted to rescue him).

Actionability

[Add to the end of n.78]   **1–30**

See also *Greenway v Johnson Matthey Plc* [2015] P.I.Q.R. P10, appeal dismissed [2016] EWCA Civ 408 (where, in breach of duty, the defendant's employees were exposed to platinum salts in the course of their employment and thereby sensitised to allergy, they could not claim for loss of earnings or earnings capacity where no allergy had in fact developed before their exposure ceased and their condition was and would remain symptomless); also *Saunderson v Sonae Industria (UK) Ltd* [2015] EWHC 2264 (QB) (a group action involving 16,000 potential claims was dismissed where there was insufficient evidence that a plume of smoke and fumes from a fire on a site controlled by the defendants caused the claimants anything other than a transient and trifling irritation). Further, see *Long v Western Sussex Hospitals NHS Trust* [2016] EWHC 251 (QB), where a negligent delay in treatment did not leave the claimant appreciably worse off, and therefore damage had not been suffered damage for the purposes of a claim.

THE DUTY TO TAKE CARE

1.—THE CONCEPT OF A DUTY OF CARE

(B) Duty formulae

History

[*Add new footnote to text*]   **2–05**

"Cause of action" is a term that will recur throughout this work. *Per* Diplock LJ in *Letang v Cooper* [1965] 1 Q.B. 232 at 242 it is used to, "describe the various categories of factual situations which entitle[d] one person to obtain from the court a remedy against another." (quoted by Arden LJ in *Clark v In Focus Asset Management & Tax Solutions Ltd* [2014] P.N.L.R. 19, CA at [4]).

(C) Application of the Caparo analysis

Duty to the claimant

[*Note 86*]   **2–39**

Thompson v Renwick Group Plc reported at [2014] P.I.Q.R. P18, CA.

Fair, just and reasonable

[*Add new footnote n.88a after "policy" in line 1*]   **2–41**

NOTE 88a. See *Smith v University of Leicester NHS Trust* [2016] EWHC 817 (QB) where it was held not to be "fair, just and reasonable" to hold that a hospital owed a duty to diagnose a genetic disorder promptly in order that relatives of the patient could themselves be tested and treated for the disorder.

CHAPTER 2

2.—THE KIND OF CONDUCT

(B) Omissions

A case study

2–68 [*Add to n.140*]

... para.2-91]. See also *JR v Secretary of State for Justice,* County Court (Leeds) 11 March 2016 (the probation service does not owe a duty to inform a person involved in a relationship with someone assessed as posing a risk of violence, of their offending history and the risks that they pose).

2–68a [*Add new paragraph to text*]

A duty of care on the basis of a failure to protect the claimant from a foreseeable danger arising from a source external to the defendants themselves, was also rejected in *ABC v St George's Healthcare NHS Foundation Trust.*[140a] The claimant's father was detained under s.37 of the Mental Health Act 1983 at a hospital run by the first defendant, where he was seen by a social worker employed by the second defendant. In the course of his detention a diagnosis that he was suffering from Huntingdon's disease was confirmed by the third defendant. The disease is genetic in origin and there was therefore a 50% chance it had been passed to the claimant, who was pregnant. Her father refused to give permission for the information to be communicated to her, but she subsequently found out accidentally and brought proceedings alleging negligence and consequent psychiatric injury. In striking the claim out as disclosing no reasonable cause of action it was said that there had been no assumption of responsibility by the defendants to the claimant, no special relationship existed between them and her, and it would not be fair, just and reasonable to impose a duty of care.

NOTE 140a. [2015] P.I.Q.R. P18, Nicol J.

Known dangers

2–71 [*Add to n.143*]

... 485.] See also *Coope v Ward* [2015] EWCA Civ 30 (neighbouring landowners owed each other a measured duty of care in respect of the consequences of the collapse of a wall between their adjoining properties, even though the collapse itself did not arise as a result their fault; nevertheless it was not fair, just and reasonable to impose on one party a liability to contribute to the cost of some as yet unspecified engineering solution and in particular it was unreasonable to compel that party to contribute to the construction of a wall which was entirely on the other's land and from which they would derive no benefit other than the removal of the risk of a further collapse).

Inducing reliance

2–80 [*Note 179*]

Thompson v Renwick Group Plc reported at [2014] P.I.Q.R. P18, CA.

[*Add new footnote 179a to "subsidiary" in the last line*]   **2–82**

NOTE 179a. Subsequently, in *Lungowe v Vedanta Resources plc* [2016] EWHC 975 (TCC) it was accepted that Arden LJ's four criteria could be used to found a duty between third parties affected by the activities of a subsidiary and the parent company. Whilst "a claim is more likely to succeed if advanced by former employees" it is the case that "claims made by residents, rather than former employees, are still arguable" (para.[115]).

Voluntary assumption

[*Add to n.214*]   **2–95**

[2011] 1 F.L.R. 1361, CA,] Chap 12, para.12-18, below.

[*Add to n.215*]

... of the charge).] See also *Sebry v Companies House* [2015] EWHC 115 (QB) where it was held that the registrar of companies owed a duty of care when entering a winding-up order on the companies register, to take reasonable care to ensure that the order was not registered against the wrong company. (The claimant company was wrongly recorded on the register as having been wound up by order of the court when it was not in liquidation; its suppliers then withdrew credit and it was subsequently placed in administration).

3.—THE KIND OF HARM

(A) Introduction

[*Note 223*]   **2–100**

Robinson v Chief Constable of West Yorkshire reported at [2014] P.I.Q.R. P14, CA.

(B) Physical damage claims

Physical change

[*Add to the end of n.229*]   **2–102**

See also *Greenway v Johnson Matthey Plc* [2016] EWCA Civ 408, Ch.1, para.1-30, above.

Engaging with the enemy

[*Add to note 258*]   **2–114**

... 130 L.Q.R. 28]; also Fairgrieve, "Suing the military: the justiciability of damages claims against the armed forces" C.L.J. 2014, 73(1), 18.

Police operations

[*Note 264*]   **2–117**

Robinson v Chief Constable of West Yorkshire reported at [2014] P.I.Q.R. P14, CA.

CHAPTER 2

[Add new footnote 266a to "claimant" in the last line]

NOTE 266a. See also *Rathband v Chief Constable of Northumbria* [2016] EWHC 181 (QB), para.2-311, below.

Abstraction of water

2–119 *[Add to n.269]*

... 1 W.L.R. 161]; also *Chetwynd v Tunmore* [2016] EWHC 156 (QB), Ch.13, para.13-58, below.

(C) Psychiatric injury

Intentionally inflicted mental injury

2–130a *[Add new paragraph to text]*

In *O v A*,[298a] the Supreme Court considered whether the publication of a semi-autobiographical book by a celebrity graphically disclosing past incidents of abuse, where such disclosures would cause harm to the defendant's autistic infant son, would fall within the rule in *Wilkinson v Downton*. It was held that the tort of wilful infringement of the right to personal safety (as the tort in *Wilkinson v Downton* should be known) has three elements; a conduct element; a mental element; and a consequence element.[298b] The conduct element "requires words or conduct directed towards the claimant for which there is no justification or reasonable excuse".[298c] In general "it is difficult to envisage any circumstances in which speech which is not deceptive, threatening or possibly abusive, could give rise to liability in tort," and the true words published in the instant case could not constitute the conduct element of the tort.[298d] The mental element requires the claimant to demonstrate that the defendant had an actual "intention to cause physical harm or severe mental or emotional distress".[298e] Recklessness will not suffice, and imputed intention has "no proper role in the modern law of tort".[298f] The consequence element requires that the claimant demonstrate that they have suffered physical harm or recognised psychiatric illness as a result of the conduct. The continuing utility of the tort, in doubt following the judgment of Lord Hoffmann in Wainwright which suggested that Wilkinson had "no leading role in the modern law," was confirmed,[298g] as "negligence and intent are very different fault elements and there are principled reasons for differentiating between the bases (and possible extent) of liability for causing personal injury in either case".[298h]

NOTE 298a. [2016] A.C. 219. See, Hunt, "*Wilkinson v Downton* revisited" C.L.J. 2015, 74(3), 392.

NOTE 298b. para.[88].

NOTE 298c. para.[74].

NOTE 298d. para.[77].

NOTE 298e. para.[87].

NOTE 298f. para.[81].

NOTE 298g. *Wainwright v Home Office* [2004] 2 AC 406, 425, para.[41].

NOTE 298h. *O v A* para.[63].

Proximity in time and space

[Add to end of n.336]   **2–153**

See also *Young v MacVean* [2015] CSIH 70; 2015 S.L.T. 729 where it was held that a parent who perceived the immediate aftermath of an accident involving her child without being aware, until later, of her child's involvement, could not recover for psychiatric injury suffered as a result of her later knowledge. She had not perceived, with her own unaided senses, the aftermath of the negligent imperilment of a person with whom she shared a close tie of love and affection, and therefore could not recover.

[Add to the end of n.339]

; *Baker v Cambridgeshire and Peterborough NHS Foundation Trust* [2015] EWHC 609 (QB) at [41].

Later consequences of accident

[Add new paragraph to text]   **2–154a**

Taylor v A Novo was applied in *Wild v Southend University Hospital NHS Foundation Trust.*[341a] A father suffered psychiatric injury due to his presence during the stillbirth of his child, although he had not been present at the time of the negligence that led to the death of the foetus in the womb. His claim for damages for psychiatric injury therefore failed, as he was not present to witness the shocking event in question, but had only a witnessed the consequence of the injury sustained at that time. The mother was able to recover for her psychiatric injury and it might be thought unsatisfactory to have in effect a gender divide in pre-natal negligence cases, with mothers being able to recover damages, and fathers frequently not, albeit suffering a similar injury. Further, taken with *Taylor*, the case illustrates that it is easier to recover for psychiatric injury sustained as a result of witnessing injuries caused by an accident, rather than witnessing injuries resulting from industrial diseases or clinical negligence, where those injuries may not become apparent until years after the event.
NOTE 341a. [2014] EWHC 4053 (QB), Michael Kent QC (sitting as a Judge of the High Court). See Allen, "Nervous shock: a "most vexed and tantalising topic" . . . still" 2015 J.P.I.L. (1), 1.

Shock-induced injury

[Add to n.345]   **2–156**

See further *Liverpool Women's Hospital NHS Foundation Trust v Ronayne* [2015] EWCA Civ 588, n.350, below (no "horrifying event" where the appearance of the claimant's wife when he saw her in hospital before and after surgery was not exceptional by objective standards); Macpherson, "Secondary victims" Rep. B. 2015, 126.

Suddenness

[Add to n.347]   **2–157**

. . . P329, CA.] See also *Young v Macvean* 2015 S.L.T. 729, IH, para.2-153, above (a mother who passed the scene of a running down accident and saw the damage to the vehicle which had struck a pedestrian, not knowing that the pedestrian was her son and that he had suffered fatal injuries, was not a secondary victim since her psychiatric illness was not the result of a sudden appreciation of the shocking event which caused his death).

[*Add to n.349*]

There was no sudden and direct appreciation of a horrifying event where the claimant, over a period of time, was informed in telephone messages or in a face-to face conversation with her sister's husband, of her sister's deteriorating, and ultimately fatal, medical condition: *Shorter v Surrey and Sussex Healthcare NHS Trust* [2015] EWHC 614 (QB) (*per* Swift J., it was necessary to be cautious in finding that when the claimant saw her sister on a hospital trolley towards the start of the period she was in hospital, the claimant's professional expertise as a nurse made the sight more horrifying than it would have been to a person without her knowledge: the "event" had to be one that would be recognised as horrifying by a person of ordinary susceptibility; in other words, by objective standards).

2–158   [*Add to n.350*]

Contrast *Liverpool Women's Hospital NHS Foundation Trust v Ronayne* [2015] EWCA Civ 588 (no "seamless tale" where over the period of time the claimant's wife was in hospital there was a series of events as her condition deteriorated and in advance of two particularly distressing visits he was given information in advance of what to expect).

Work-related stress

2–167   [*Add to n.366 after the reference to Dickins v O2 Plc*]

. . . [2009] I.R.L.R. 58, CA]; *Daniel v Secretary of State for the Department of Health* [2014] EWHC 2578 (QB); *Yapp v Foreign and Commonwealth Office* [2015] I.R.L.R. 112, CA. [See generally . . .

(E) Negligent statements causing financial injury

Hedley Byrne & Co Ltd v Heller & Partners Ltd

2–181   [*Add footnote reference 402A to "negligence" in line 12 at the top of page[87]*]

NOTE 402a. See Campbell, "The absence of negligence in *Hedley Byrne v Heller*" L.Q.R. 2016, 132(Apr), 266.

Reasonable reliance

2–194   [*Add new n.425a to "reliance"in the sub-heading*]

NOTE 425a. This paragraph was considered by Lord Brodie, dissenting in part, in *NRAM plc v Bell & Scott LLP* [2016] CSIH 11; 2016 S.L.T. 285.

[*Add to text after n.428*]

. . . even though it was gratuitous.[428].] It has also been held that it would be reasonable for a commercial lender such as a bank to rely on statements from a solicitor regarding the affairs of their mutual client, the effect of which were to leave a substantial debt unsecured, without checking the accuracy of such information, and a competent solicitor should have foreseen such reliance. A solicitor could not avoid responsibility for a serious error just because the recipients of the statement could have easily discovered that truth rather than relying on what a trustworthy professional told them.[428a]

Note 428a. *NRAM plc v Bell & Scott LLP*, n.425a, above.

[*Add to text after n.431*]

There can be no true reliance where the statement which forms the basis of the claim does not come into existence until after the claimant has taken the action said to have be taken in reliance on it.[431a] So, claims against property consultants based on defects in properties for which certificates of proper construction had been provided, failed, the leaseholders having purchased their interest in the properties before the certificates were seen by them: that being so they could not have relied on any negligent misstatement the certificates contained at the time they committed themselves to purchase.[431b]

Note 431a. *Hunt v Optima (Cambridge) Ltd* [2014] P.N.L.R. 29, CA.
Note 431b. Ibid.

Proximity of relationship

[*Add to the end of n.432*]   2–195

See also *Playboy Club London Ltd v Banca Nazionale Del Lavoro SpA* [2016] EWCA Civ 457 (there is no relationship of proximity between a bank and an undisclosed principal, so whilst a duty may be owed to the agent, it will not be owed to the principal). See further, Ch.9, para.9-84.

[*Add to the end of n.433*]

See *Swynson Ltd v Lowick Rose LLP* [2014] P.N.L.R. 27, para.2-204a, below (no duty owed to a director of a company in respect of advice given to that company).

Company auditors

[*Add new footnote 445a to "company" in the last line*]   2–199

Note 445a. An auditor engaged to carry out non-statutory audits may owe a duty to third parties other than the members of a company in general meeting, see *Barclays Bank plc v Grant Thornton UK LLP* [2015] EWHC 320 *per* Cooke J at [50]-[54], although on the facts no duty was owed in light of a disclaimer inserted into the audit reports produced by the defendant.

Company directors

[*Add new paragraph to text*]   2–204a

A situation which can be seen as the converse of *Williams v Natural Life Health Foods Ltd*[454a] arose in *Swynson Ltd v Lowick Rose LLP*,[454b] where the defendant accountants firm were held not to owe a personal duty to a company director in respect of advice given to the company, notwithstanding that it was foreseeable that the director may suffer loss as a result of negligent advice

given by them. It makes no difference if the company has a single owner who is also the director of the company.
NOTE 454a. [1998] 1 W.L.R. 830, HL.
NOTE 454b. [2014] P.N.L.R. 27.

2–206   [*Add new footnote reference 456a to "obscure" in the last line*]
NOTE 456a. The approach in *Williams v Natural Life Health Foods Ltd* was applied in preference to *Merrett v Babb* in *Summit Advances Ltd v Bush* [2015] P.N.L.R. 18 (mortgage lenders were unsuccessful in their contention that a surveyor employed by a limited liability partnership owed them a personal duty of care in relation to a valuation of property prepared by him in the course of that employment).

Disclaimers

2–213   [*Add to text after n.482*]

In *Barclays Bank plc v Grant Thornton UK LLP*[482a] a disclaimer appearing on the first page of a non-statutory audit report, which followed a standard form produced by the Institute of Chartered Accountants in England & Wales in respect of statutory audits, save for changing "the company's members" to "the company's director[s]", was held sufficient to prevent a duty of care arising to the third party bank.
NOTE 482a. [2015] EWHC 320, para.2-199, above.

Unfair Contract Terms Act 1977

2–214   [*Add new footnote reference 482a after "1977" in the heading*]

NOTE 482a. Where one party is a consumer and the other is a trader the Unfair Contract Terms Act 1977 ceases to have effect for contracts made after 1st October 2015 and is replaced by the Consumer Rights Act 2015. The Unfair Terms in Consumer Contracts Regulation 1999 are also repealed, and the provisions consolidated with the consumer provisions of the Unfair Contract Terms Act in Pt.2 of the Consumer Rights Act. Terms which seek to exclude or restrict liability in respect of personal injury or death are void (s.65). Other terms which seek to exclude liability in negligence, for example for property damage or economic loss, are subject to a test of fairness (s.62). The Act provides guidance on the meaning of unfairness (ss. 62, 63 and sch. 2). The Unfair Contract Terms Act will continue to apply to contracts made between two businesses in a modified form. The amendments to the 1977 Act are set out in Sch. 4 of the Consumer Rights Act. A Legislative Note summarising the effect of the new provisions appears in Appendix A to this Supplement.

[*Delete text of n.483 after the first sentence*]

[*Add new footnote reference 486a to "factors" in line 12*]

NOTE 486a. See also *Barclays Bank plc v Grant Thornton UK LLP* [2015] EWHC 320, *per* Cooke J at [55] to [91].

2–215   [*Add to text at the end of the paragraph*]

Likewise a disclaimer was successful in limiting a duty of care owed to a third party bank in relation to two non-statutory audit reports where the commercial strength of the parties meant that they were both able to protect their own interests.[487a]

Note 487a. *Barclays Bank plc v Grant Thornton UK LLP* [2015] EWHC 320, Cooke J., para.2-199, above (considering the reasonableness test in s.2 of the 1977 Act). See further, Ch.9, para.9-38, below.

(F) Negligent conduct causing financial injury

Third party payments

[*Add new footnote 490a to"reasonable" in the last line*]   **2–219**

Note 490a. See further, *Network Rail Infrastructure Ltd v Handy* [2015] EWHC 1175 (TCC).

Balancing policy concerns

[*Add to n.518*]   **2–233**

See also *Sebry v Companies House* [2015] EWHC 115 (QB), Edis J., n.215, above (in imposing a duty of care upon the register of companies in relation to the accuracy of an entry on the companies register a number of factors came into account, notably that: (a) unless a remedy was provided by the common law of negligence, a company damaged by carelessness in the particular circumstances would have no remedy; (b) it was not difficult for the registrar's staff to avoid errors of the type made; (c) there were no public policy reasons for denying a duty of care; (d) the statutory duty or contractual relationship between the company and the registrar did not limit the nature and extent of the responsibility; (e) balancing the harm done to the company against the potential adverse impact on the registrar, it was clear that the balance favoured the loss falling on the registrar rather than the company; (f) it was likely that the imposition of a duty would improve the accuracy of the register, which was plainly in the public interest. *Sebry* was distinguished by Master Matthews in *Chief Land Registrar v Caffery & Co* [2016] EWHC 161 (Ch), where it was held that a firm of solicitors did not owe a duty to a bank to check statements made by clients leading to the unwarranted discharge of a mortgage, as a solicitor is only required to "do all such things on the client's instructions as [he] believes to be proper and lawful."

Other third party claimants

[*Add to n.529*]   **2–238**

. . . 2 Lloyd's Rep. 249, CA]; also *Caliendo v Mishcon de Reya* [2016] EWHC 150 (Ch) (solicitors acting for a football club's holding company on the claimants sale of their controlling interest in the club, owed a limited duty of care to the claimants albeit not retained by them, but on the facts were not in breach of that duty).

Miscellaneous cases

[*Add to text after n.555*]   **2–246**

. . . to speak.[555] An employer does not owe a duty to employees to prevent the development of a condition not amounting to physical injury where this may lead to reduced earning capacity.[555a]

NOTE 555a. *Greenway v Johnson Matthey plc* [2016] EWCA Civ 408 in particular at [46]-[51].

2–247 [*Add new footnote reference 555b to "relevant" in line 1*]

NOTE 555b. See further paras. 2-298 and 2-329 below and Ch.12, paras. 12-05ff.

[*Note 558*]

Harrison v Technical Sign Co Ltd reported at [2014] P.N.L.R. 15.

[*Add to n.558*]

... shop front).] See also *Stagecoach South Western Trains v Hind* [2014] E.G.L.R. 59, Ch.9, para.9-311, below.

4.—THE KIND OF CLAIMANT

(A) Introduction

Extra sensitive claimants

2–269 [*Add to n.614*]

... 69 C.L.J. 435]; Keren-Paz, "Liability for consequences, duty of care and the limited relevance of specific reliance: new insights on *Bhamra v Dubb*" (2016) 1 PN 50.

(C) Unborn children

Congenital Disabilities (Civil Liability) Act 1976

2–281 [*Add new footnote reference 643a to "mother" in line 5*]

NOTE 643a. See *per* Lord Dyson MR in *CP v Criminal Injuries Compensation Authority* [2015] 2 W.L.R. 463, CA, Ch.17, para.17-33 below, at [66]: " ... in English law women do not owe a duty of care in tort to their unborn child. A competent woman cannot be forced to have a caesarean section or other medical treatment to prevent potential risk to the foetus during childbirth. The negligent acts of a third party tortfeasor, which inflict harm on an unborn child, are actionable by the child on birth if the child is born with disabilities under s.1(1) of the Congenital Disabilities (Civil Liability) Act 1976 . But claims cannot be brought under this Act against the child's mother unless (by s.2) the harm is caused by her when she is driving a motor vehicle." He went on to say, in the context of a claim for criminal injuries compensation, "The law would be incoherent if a child were unable to claim compensation from her mother for breach of a duty of care owed during pregnancy, but the mother was criminally liable for causing the harm which gave rise to damage and a right to compensation under the 1995 Act."

[*Add to n.644*]

For the position where a child *in utero,* injured by its mother, seeks compensation under the Criminal Injuries Compensation Scheme, see Ch.17, para.17-33, below.

5.—THE KIND OF DEFENDANT

(E) Public bodies

The police

2–311

[Add to n.704]

In *B v Chief Constable of X* [2015] I.R.L.R. 284, Males J., it was observed that a Chief Constable owed a duty of care to an officer operating undercover to take reasonable steps to ensure that he did not suffer psychiatric injury as a result of the stress of his work; but there was no breach of duty on the facts, and the injury alleged by the claimant arose from his own misconduct.

[Note 707]

Robinson v Chief Constable of West Yorkshire reported at [2014] P.I.Q.R. P14, CA.

[Add to text after n.707]

Despite the general duty of care owed by the police as a quasi-employer to officers as quasi-employees, the police do not owe a duty of care to police officers injured by the actions of criminals during the carrying out of core operation functions under pressure, as the imposition of such duties may give rise to defensive policing.[707a] Whilst this may bear harshly on officers injured during operations, it was fair, just and reasonable, given the public interest in the police performing their functions fearlessly and with dispatch. Further, a duty of care in relation to the planning and execution of an operation involving firearms officers was not owed to the operation's main subject, where there was no lack of care in the selection of the firearms officers and the police had not assumed responsibility to him.[707b]

NOTE 707a. *Rathband v Chief Constable of Northumbria* [2016] EWHC 181 (QB), Males J. (It was not fair, just and reasonable to impose a duty to take immediate steps to warn a police officer that a fugitive offender, who was known already to have killed one person and injured another, had rung 999 and uttered threats against police officers generally, saying that he was "coming to get you.") See further, Ch.11, para.11-74, below.

NOTE 707b. *Davis v Commissioner of Police of the Metropolis* [2016] EWHC 38 (QB).

Hill and Smith

[Delete text in n.710 after the first line and replace as follows]

2–312

. . . *South Wales Police*] [2015] A.C. 1732, para.2-312a, below.

[Add new paragraph to text]

2–312a

In *Michael v Chief Constable of South Wales*[710a] the Supreme Court confirmed the continuing applicability of the decision in *Smith*. The appellants were the parents and children of the deceased, who had been murdered by her ex-partner despite making an emergency call to the police, to which it was alleged they had failed to respond to appropriately. In the lead judgment Lord Toulson JSC held that the police did not owe a duty of care, even in circumstances where they were aware of a serious threat to an individual (which they know from the content of the deceased's emergency call) or from a particular individual (which they should also have known from the call). Imposing such duties would not be fair, just and reasonable, would lead to increased resource pressures on police forces without necessarily leading to corresponding improvements in performance, and limits on the scope of the duties would be difficult fairly to identify. Further, such duties were not compelled by art.2 of the European Convention on Human Rights, which does not require that individuals be compensated through claims in negligence in circumstances which may well also give rise to compensation for breach of the Convention. Further there was no duty owed by virtue of an assumption of responsibility. However, the claim for damages under s.7 of the Human Rights Act 1998 could proceed.[710b]

NOTE 710a. [2015] A.C. 1732. See Goudkamp, "A revolution in duty of care?" L.Q.R. 2015, 131(Oct), 519; McBride, "Michael and the future of tort law" (2016) 1 PN 14, Tofaris and Steel, "Negligence liability for omissions and the police" C.L.J. 2016, 75(1), 128.

NOTE 710b. See generally para.2-346, below.

2–313a [Add new paragraph to text]

There is no duty owed by police to potential witnesses in general, absent a specific assumption of responsibility. So, where witnesses to a shooting incident had given written statements to the police and, having received threats, moved house, no duty was owed to them not to reveal the new address in the course of seeking a summons to compel them to attend court proceedings. Service of the summons, and preparation of the evidence to support the application formed part of the core function of the police in obtaining and preserving evidence, protected by the principle in *Hill*. There had been no assumption of responsibility to the claimants. Their reliance on the negligent transmission of the information to the prosecuting authority could not establish liability since it formed part of preparing a police officer to give evidence in support of the application for a warrant and to hold the police liable for that communication would outflank the immunity to which they were entitled in relation to the evidence once given in court. The police were immune from action in respect of the transmission of the statement, even though it had been carried out negligently.[712a]

NOTE 712a. *CLG v Chief Constable of Merseyside* [2015] EWCA Civ 836.

The probation service

2–317 [Add new n.725a to "trial" in the last line]

NOTE 725a. For UK consideration of the liability for the probation service see *JR v Secretary of State for Justice*, County Court (Leeds) 11 March 2016, above para.2-68.

Social Welfare Officers.

[Add to n.737]   **2–320**

The decision of the Court of Appeal in *JD* has not been impliedly overruled by *Mitchell v Glasgow* [2009] UKHL 11, [2009] 1 A.C. 874 and *Michael v Chief Constable of South Wales* [2015] UKSC 2, [2015] A.C. 1732 and remains binding authority at the level of the Court of Appeal for the proposition that social workers owe a duty of care to children to protect them from abuse of which they are aware: *CN v Poole Borough Council* [2016] EWHC 569 (QB)).

Fire services

[Add to n.742]   **2–323**

For the position in Scotland see *Mackay v Scottish Fire & Rescue Service* [2015] CSOH 55 (no duty owed to a pedestrian injured by ice falling from a tenement roof after the defender had inspected the property to establish the risk of injury posed by ice and snow which had built up on its façade: the firefighters had neither caused the situation nor made it worse and there was no assumption of responsibility to a pedestrian passing below); also *A J Allan (Blairnyle) Ltd v Strathclyde Fire Board* [2016] CSIH 3; 2016 S.L.T. 253 (no duty owed to the owner of property when the fire service had attended and seemingly extinguished a fire, but had negligently carried out damping down operations and failed to use thermal imaging to identify that the fire remained residually active, the property being destroyed after they left the scene). See Macpherson, "From a little spark" Reparation Bulletin. 2016. 128. 4.

Other cases

[Add new paragraph to text]   **2–324a**

A sewerage operator did not assume responsibility towards a customer in circumstances where it had engaged in the clean-up of escaped sewage from her home, because its actions did not go beyond that which was required by the statutory scheme under the Water Industry Act 1991.[748a]
NOTE 748a. *Nicholson v Thames Water Utilities Ltd* [2014] EWHC 4249 (QB), Ch.13, para.13-90, below.

Negligence and misfeasance

[Add to n.755]   **2–326**

... 2861, CA.] *Rowley* was applied in *Lillian Darby (Administratrix) v Richmond upon Thames LBC* [2015] EWHC 909 (QB) (a local housing authority performing its statutory duty to allocate social housing by assessing need under a points system, owed no duty of care in applying that system to the deceased, who had made a request with the support of his GP, to be re-housed since he suffered from leukaemia and was at risk of infection if he continued to live in his existing accommodation with his sister and her baby: his need was not assessed as urgent and he contracted influenza and died three weeks later).

CHAPTER 2

[*Add to text after n.755*]

... payments.[755] The Human Embryology and Fertilisation Authority were held not to owe a duty of care in negligence in respect of its regulatory activities, in part because a claim in misconduct would exist if bad faith on the part of HEFA were shown, and in the absence of bad faith the Human Fertilisation and Embryology Act 1990 provided adequate avenues to challenge the decision of HEFA.[755a]

NOTE 755a. *Human Fertilisation and Embryology Authority v ARGC Ltd* [2016] EWHC 460 (QB).

Planning and building regulation

2-327   [*Add to text after n.759*]

... planning or building regulation.[759] So, liability attached in negligence where a local authority responded to a search request from a developer of land to the effect that parking spaces which formed part of the property were not highway maintainable at public expense, when, after the land had been purchased, it transpired they were.[759a] [But, seemingly something more is required ...

NOTE 759a. *Chesterton Commercial (Oxon) Ltd v Oxfordshire CC* [2015] EWHC 2020 (Ch) (the developer recovered the value of the parking spaces, costs incurred in attempting to obtain a stopping up order, and increased borrowing costs following upon its overpayment for the property).

Child abuse cases

2-331   [*Add new footnote reference 767a to "Appeal" in the last line on page* [148]]

NOTE 767a. In *CN v Poole BC* [2016] EWHC 569 (QB), Slade J set aside an order striking out the claims of two children who alleged that a local authority had negligently failed to exercise its powers under the Children Act 1989 to protect them from abuse. In so doing she relied upon the decision of the CA in *D v East Berkshire NHS Trust* [20034] Q.B. 558, which was not the subject of the later appeal to the House of Lords. She did not accept the submission that the CA's decision had implicitly been overruled by *Mitchell v Glasgow City Council* [2009] 1 A.C. 874, para.2-347, below or *Michael v Chief Constable of South Wales* [2015] A.C. 1732, para.2-312, above.

[*Add to n.768*]

See also *Williams v Hackney LBC* [2015] EWHC 2629 (QB).

Other articles

2-341   [*Add to text after n.785*]

The police were held to have violated their duty under art.3 in circumstances where there had been serious systemic failings in the investigation of a series of over 100 serious sexual assaults committed by the same individual.[785a]

NOTE 785a. *DSD v Commissioner of Police for the Metropolis* [2016] Q.B. 161 (the defendant has received permission to appeal to the Supreme Court).

CHAPTER 3

PARTIES AND VICARIOUS LIABILITY

1.—PARTIES

(A) The Crown

Liability for negligence

[Add to text after n.34] **3–11**

Since s.2 of the Crown Proceedings Act 1947 was designed to put the Crown in the same position as an ordinary private person of full age and capacity, the Home Office can be liable, by way of a non-delegable duty of care,[34a] for the negligent actions of an independent contractor.[34b]

NOTE 34a. In relation to such duties see para.3-195, below and *Woodland v Essex County Council* [2013] 3 W.L.R. 1227, S.C.

NOTE 34b. *GB v Home Office* [2015] EWHC 819 (QB), Coulson J, para.3-196, below.

(B) Judges and quasi judges, prosecutors, the police

Judicial acts

[Add to n.42] **3–15**

An ombudsman appointed under the Financial Services and Markets Act 2000 to determine disputes between consumers and providers of financial services makes a judicial decision when making an award, see *Clark v In Focus Asset Management & Tax Solutions Ltd* [2014] P.N.L.R. 19, CA, *per* Arden LJ at [82].

(C) The armed forces

Other cases

[Add to n.75] **3–25**

. . . should have been aware.] Contrast *Vaughan v Ministry of Defence* [2015] EWHC 1404 (QB) William Davis J. (the defendant did not owe a duty of care as employer, to a marine who suffered serious injuries after executing a shallow dive in the sea while off duty during a training week).

(H) Partners

Generally

3–54 *[Add to n.139]*

Further, see *Northampton Regional Livestock Centre Co Ltd v Cowling* [2015] EWCA Civ 651, para.3-150, n.387, below.

(J) Children

Duty of care of parents

3–58 *[Add to n.153]*

See also *O v A* [2015] E.M.L.R. 4, CA, Ch.2, para.2-130a, above (no duty of care was owed by a father to his young son, who suffered a number of significant disabilities, not to publish an account of sexual abuse the father had suffered as a child, notwithstanding that such publication would be likely to cause his son enduring psychological harm). Appeal, on different grounds, allowed [2016] A.C. 219.

(K) Prisoners and bankrupts

Prisoners

3–68 *[Note 176]*

Cox v Ministry of Justice reported at [2014] P.I.Q.R. P17, CA.

Bankrupt's capacity to sue

3–71a *[Add new paragraph to text]*

A trustee in bankruptcy does not owe a common law duty of care to a bankrupt in managing the bankrupt's estate and realising assets. A trustee was not liable to a bankrupt against whom a bankruptcy order had been made which was annulled due to serious procedural irregularities. The bankrupt had rightly claimed throughout that she had sufficient assets to satisfy all judgments, but it was no part of the trustee's role to review judgments or orders which at the time appeared to have been properly made.[185a]

NOTE 185a. *Oraki v Bramston* [2015] EWHC 2046 (Ch). *Per* Proudman J at [33]: " . . . it would be inconsistent with the requirement that the permission of the court must be given if the bankrupt had an unfettered right to take proceedings against his trustee. In any event there is no need for the bankrupt to have a general right of action based on a common law duty which would conflict with the statutory regime of rights, for example, s.303, 304, 325 (2), 326(3) and 363" (of the Insolvency Act 1986).

(L) Persons suffering mental disorder

Generally

[Add new paragraph to text]   3–75a

The extent to which, if at all, profound mental disorder could prevent an individual being in breach of a duty of care was explored in *Dunnage v Randall*.[192a] The claimant suffered serious injuries in attempting unsuccessfully to prevent his uncle, who suffered disabling mental illness, from setting fire to himself. He sought to recover damages on the basis that his uncle was in breach of a duty of care towards him as a potential rescuer. On appeal it was held that, the test being objective, liability attached. A defendant impaired by medical problems, whether physical or mental, could not escape liability if he caused injury by failing to exercise reasonable care. Only a defendant whose medical incapacity had the effect of entirely eliminating any fault or responsibility for an injury to another could be excused, but that was not the position where, as here, the defendant's mind, although deluded, directed his actions.

NOTE 192a. [2016] P.I.Q.R. P1, CA, Ch.1, para.1-10, above.

2.—VICARIOUS LIABILITY

(A) Employees and relationships akin to employment

Introduction

[Add to n.259]   3–105

... C.L.J. 17]; Mackay, "Vicarious liability: there's an app for that" J.P.I. Law 2016, 2, 90; Morgan, "Vicarious liability for group companies: the final frontier of vicarious liability?" (2015) 4 PN 276.

Who is an employee?

[Add new footnote reference 259a to "significance" in line 4]   3–107

NOTE 259a. See Morgan, "Vicarious liability for independent contractors?" (2015) 4 PN 235 (considers whether vicarious liability can be extended to encompass the fault of an independent contractor).

Illustrations: unskilled occupations

*[Delete text from "A prisoner..." in line 7 to the end of the paragraph   3–113
including the text of n.282 and replace as follows]*

The Ministry of Justice were vicariously liable for the negligent acts of a prisoner engaging in paid employment within the prison kitchens.[282]
NOTE 282. *Cox v Ministry of Justice* [2016] UKSC 10; [2016] 2 W.L.R. 806, SC, para.3-118a, below.

Relationships akin to employment

[Add new paragraph to text]   3–118a

The approach to vicarious liability set out in the *Christian Brothers* case[304a] has been further considered by the Supreme Court in *Cox v Ministry of*

Justice.[304b] The claimant, a catering manager in a prison, was injured as a result of the negligence of a prisoner carrying out duties in the kitchen, for which he was paid a modest wage. The Ministry argued that the relationship between the Prison Service and prisoners was very different from an employer/employee relationship in that the Prison Service's primary purpose was not a business or profit, but prisoners' rehabilitation, and prisoners had no interest in furthering the Prison Service's objectives. It was always necessary to ask whether it would be fair, just and reasonable to impose vicarious liability; and there was a risk of further claims arising should vicarious liability be imposed. These arguments were rejected. It was said to be no bar to liability that the defendant was not carrying on a commercial activity, or that it was not deriving profit from the tortfeasor's activities. It was sufficient that there was a defendant carrying on activities in furtherance of its own interests. Prisoners working in the kitchens were integrated into the operation of the prison, so that the activities assigned to them by the Prison Service formed an integral part of the activities it carried on, in particular the activity of providing meals for prisoners. The prisoners were placed in a position where there was a risk that they could commit a variety of negligent acts within the field of activities assigned to them, they worked under the direction of prison staff and the claimant had been injured as a result of negligence when the prisoner was carrying on the activities assigned to him. The fact that setting prisoners to work was one means by which the Prison Service sought to rehabilitate prisoners did not alter that conclusion. The fact that prison operators were under a statutory duty to provide prisoners with useful work was not incompatible with vicarious liability being imposed. Where the criteria[304c] in the Christian Brothers case were satisfied it would not generally be necessary to reassess the fairness of the result.

NOTE 304a. [2013] 2 A.C. 1, para.3-118, above.

NOTE 304b. [2016] UKSC 10; [2016] 2 W.L.R. 806, SC. The leading judgment was given by Lord Reed SCJ with whom the other members of the court agreed. See also, *Mohamud v WM Morrison Supermarkets Plc* [2016] UKSC 11, para.3-153, below.

NOTE 304c. Lord Reed's judgment emphasises that not all of the criteria set out by Lord Phillips' in the Christian Brothers case are of equal significance. In particular the presence or absence of insurance, and the issue of control are likely to be less important than the others, although given the possibility of many variations on the facts, they cannot be excluded.

3–118b   *[Add new paragraph to text]*

In contrast, the Christian Brothers criteria did not avail the claimant in *NA v Nottinghamshire CC*[304d] in which it was alleged that the local authority was vicariously liable for the actions of foster parents in physically and sexually abusing the claimant who the authority had placed in their care.[304e] The Court of Appeal disagreed, holding that the relationship between foster parents and the local authority was a more distant one than that between the lay brothers and the Institute in the earlier case. It was not "closely akin to employment". In the words of Tomlinson LJ:

> "The provision of family life is not and by definition cannot be part of the activity of the local authority or of the enterprise upon which it is engaged. Family life is not

capable of being so regarded, precisely because inherent in it is a complete absence of external control over the imposition or arrangement of day to day family routine, save insofar as is provided by the general law or by ordinary social conventions. The control retained by the local authority is at a higher or macro level. Micro management of the day to day family life of foster children, or of their foster parents in the manner in which they create the day to day family environment, would be inimical to that which fostering sets out to achieve . . . The control retained by the local authority, over and above the proper selection of foster parents and adequate supervision of the placement which is here not in issue, is thus irrelevant to the risk of abuse occurring during the unregulated course of life in the foster home."[304f]

In effect a local authority is likely to be vicariously liable to a child injured as a result of negligence within a local authority care home, but not if the child is injured whilst placed in foster care.

NOTE 304d. [2015] EWCA Civ 1139; [2016] Fam. Law 171, CA. Tomlinson LJ emphasised that the case arose in a statutory framework which pre-dated the Children Act 1989. See further Gumbel QC, "Developments in vicarious liability: a practitioner's perspective" (2015) 4 PN 218.

NOTE 304e. It had already been established that the authority had not itself been negligent in placing the claimant with the foster carers in question, or in supervising the placement.

NOTE 304f. [2015] EWCA Civ 1139 at [15]. See further, para.3-196a, below.

Dishonesty, fraud or other criminal act

[Add to the end of n.387]   3–150

The test in the *Dubai Aluminium* case was considered in *Northampton Regional Livestock Centre Co Ltd v Cowling* [2015] EWCA Civ 651, a claim against partners, where the issue was the liability of both partners for a breach of duty by one of them. It was observed that in such circumstances authority was not the touchstone for joint and several partnership liability. The touchstone was the connection between the wrongful conduct and the acts a partner was authorised to do, and in particular whether the connection was such that the wrongful conduct might fairly and properly be regarded as done by the partner while acting in the ordinary course of the partnership business.

[Add to n.397]   3–153

Following *Maga*, trustees of a society of Jehovah's Witnesses were vicariously liable for sexual assaults carried out by a ministerial servant on a child in the congregation, and for the failure of the elders to take reasonable steps to protect her from the abuser once they knew of his earlier abuse of another child: *A v Trustees of the Watchtower Bible and Tract Society* [2015] EWHC 1722 (QB), Globe J.

[Add to text after n.401]

. . . racist views[401]] nor was an employer vicariously liable where a bodyshop employee sprayed a co-worker's overalls with thinning agent, an inflammable substance, and then used a cigarette lighter in his vicinity, causing serious injury.[401a] [There was an insufficiently . . .

NOTE 401a. *Graham v Commercial Bodyworks Ltd* [2015] EWCA Civ 47, considering *Vaickuviene v J Sainsbury Plc* n.401, above. While there was a risk in requiring the use of thinning agent in the course of the men's work, it could not be said that the creation of that risk was sufficiently closely connected with the highly reckless act of the guilty party.

[*Delete the last sentence of the text and the case reference in n.402*]

3–153a   [*Add new paragraph to text*]

It was otherwise where a member of a supermarket's staff, whose job was to serve customers at the store's petrol station kiosk and see that the petrol pumps and kiosk were kept in good running order, carried out a violent and unprovoked assault upon a customer who attended with an enquiry.[402] It was said in the Supreme Court that broadly two matters had to be considered: (a) what functions had been entrusted by the employer to the employee; and (b) whether there was sufficient connection between the employee's wrongful conduct and the position in which he was employed to make it right for the employer to be fixed with vicarious liability. On the facts[402a] it was the job of the member of staff concerned to attend to customers and respond to their enquiries. His conduct was inexcusable but was within the field of activities assigned to him. What happened was an unbroken sequence of events and it was not right to regard him as having metaphorically taken off his uniform when he followed the customer onto the forecourt before attacking him. Moreover, he had repeatedly told the customer to leave: that was not something personal between him and the customer; he was ordering him to keep away from his employer's premises, and he reinforced that order by violence. In doing so he was purporting to act in the furtherance of his employer's business.

NOTE 402. *Mohamud v WM Morrison Supermarkets Plc* [2016] UKSC 11.
NOTE 402a. See the analysis of Lord Toulson at [47].

Further examples of acts in the course of employment

3–156   [*Add to text after n.424*]

A bank was vicariously liable for the negligence of an employee who provided a positive reference to a third party stating that a customer had an account and was trustworthy to the extent of £1.6 million in any one week, when in fact, the customer's balance had always been nil.[424a]

NOTE 424a. *Playboy Club London Ltd v Banca Nazionale Del Lavoro SPA* [2014] EWHC 2613 (QB) the reference came from a business manager of the bank who had no responsibility for the account but the provision of a reference was deemed so closely connected with acts that she was authorised to do that the wrongful conduct might fairly and properly be regarded as done by her in the course of her employment).

3–157   [*Add to text after n.432*]

. . . he was sorting[432];] where the claimant's employee, the brother-in-law of the claimant, had convinced the defendant to provide a guarantee for a loan to a business in which they both had an interest[432a]; [where an . . .

NOTE 432a. *Bank of Ireland (UK) Plc v McLaughlin* [2015] NIQB 85.

3.—NON DELEGABLE DUTIES

(D) Special relationships

[*Note 543*]   **3–195**

Woodland v Essex CC reported at [2014] A.C. 537.

[*Add to n.543*]

See George, "Non-delegable duties of care in tort" L.Q.R. 2014, 130(Oct), 534; Morgan, "Liability for independent contractors in contract and tort: duties to ensure that care is taken" 2015 C.L.J. 74(1) 109.

[*Add note 543a to "it." in the last line*]

NOTE 543a. In *NA v Nottinghamshire County Council* [2015] EWCA Civ 1139; [2016] Fam. Law 171, CA, para.3-118b, above, it was said *per* Tomlinson LJ at [24]-[25] that, in order to be non-delegable a duty must relate to a function which the purported delegator, (on the facts the defendant local authority), had assumed a duty to perform: see para.3-196a, below.

[*Add new footnote reference 543b to "homes" in line 5*]

NOTE 543b. A detainee in an immigration removal centre run by an independent organisation on behalf of the Home Office, was owed a non-delegable duty of care in respect of allegedly negligent medical treatment received by her, since such detainees were inherently vulnerable and highly dependent on the observance of proper standards of care: *GB v Home Office* [2015] EWHC 819 (QB), Coulson J (a decision on a preliminary issue).

[*Add to n.544*]

In addition to the factors listed it must also be fair, just and reasonable to impose a non delegable duty: for a case where it was not, see *NA v Nottinghamshire CC*, above paras 3-118a, 3-195 (no such duty imposed upon a local authority in relation to acts of abuse perpetrated upon a child by foster parents with whom the child had been placed, where it would have a significant resource impact and may cause local authorities to become more unwilling to place looked after children in foster care). See *per* Black LJ at [60]-[65]; see also *VN v Brent LBC* [2016] EWHC 936 (QB), at [231].

[*Add new footnote reference 544a to "contractor" in the second last line*

NOTE 544a. The point of principle having been decided the case was remitted for trial and the claimant succeeded in establishing that her serious personal injuries were caused or materially contributed to by a breach of duty both of a lifeguard employed at the pool and a teacher, in failing to notice in time that she was in difficulties in the water: *Woodland v Maxwell* [2015] EWHC 273 (QB).

[*Add new paragraph*]   **3–196a**

Lord Sumption's five criteria were considered in *NA v Nottinghamshire CC*[545a] which has already been considered in other contexts. The claimant appealed against a decision that the defendant local authority was not in breach of a non delegable duty of care to in relation to physical and sexual abuse she had suffered at the hands of foster parents while in care. Such a duty was rejected by each of the judges in the Court of Appeal but for somewhat different reasons.

Tomlinson LJ held that the absence of the fourth criterion was crucial. In order to be non-delegable a duty must relate to a function which the purported delegator had assumed for itself a duty to perform. Fostering was a function which the local authority must, if it chooses it, entrust to others. By arranging a foster placement the local authority discharged rather than delegated its statutory duty to provide accommodation and maintenance for the child.[545b]

Burnett LJ considered that the duty which the local authority delegated was "to care for the child, to promote its welfare and to protect it from harm" so far as it reasonably could, but he did not accept that, where no vicarious liability attached,[545c] the common law should give rise to liability by an alternative route for breach of a non delegable duty where harm was deliberately inflicted.

Black LJ accepted that at least arguably all five criteria were present but held that even if that were the case it would not be fair, just and reasonable to impose a non delegable duty of care.

"It seems to me that the imposition of liability for the actions of the foster parents by means of a non-delegable duty, operating in the absence of negligence on the part of the local authority, would be likely to provoke the channelling of even more of the local authorities' scarce resources into attempting to ensure that nothing went wrong and, if such were possible, into insuring against potential liability . . . Particularly influential in my thinking is the fear that it would also lead to defensive practice in relation to the placement of children. Local authorities would inevitably become more cautious about taking the risk of placing children with foster parents and may possibly place some children who would otherwise have had the benefit of a foster home in local authority run homes instead, simply in order that the local authority can exert greater control over their day-to-day care."[545d]

NOTE 545a. [2015] EWCA Civ 1139.
NOTE 545b. at [24]. Quaere whether the coming into force of the Children Act 1989 would lead to a different conclusion, see para.3-118b, n. 304b, above.
NOTE 545c. See para.3-118a, above.
NOTE 545d. at [62].

PRINCIPAL DEFENCES AND DISCHARGES FROM LIABILITY

1.—CONTRIBUTORY NEGLIGENCE

Share in responsibility for the damage

[*Add to the end of n.66*]   **4–25**

... and *Jackson v Murray* [2015] 2 All E.R. 805, SC, para.4–40, below, *per* Lord Reed at [20]-[21].

Examples of apportionment

[*Add to text after n.70*]   **4–26**

The claimant was 60% to blame when he failed to prevent his car rolling down a hill after he had got out in order to inspect damage following an minor accident, leaving his children within the vehicle and failing to put the car in "park."[70a]
NOTE 70a. *Sparrow v Arnaud* [2016] EWHC 739 (QB).

Seat belts

[*Add to n.71*]   **4–27**

The Motor Vehicles (Wearing of Seat Belts) Regulations 1993 have been amended with effect from 1 April 2015 by the Motor Vehicles (Wearing of Seat Belts) (Amendment) (No. 2) Regulations 2015 (SI 2015/574).

Children: degree of care to be expected

[*Add to n.119*]   **4–40**

Compare *Jackson v Murray* [2015] 2 All E.R. 805, SC (the contributory negligence of a child of 13 was assessed at 50% where she stepped out from behind a school bus into the path of an oncoming car where poor light conditions made it difficult to assess the speed of the car which was too fast in the circumstances).

Intoxication

[*Add to note 144 after "railway" in the first line*]   **4–48**

... railway);] *McCaughey v Mullan* [2014] NIQB 132. [See also ...

4–50 [*Add to the last line of note 149 after the bracket*]

... of the way);] also *Scott v Gavigan* [2016] EWCA Civ 544 (pedestrian wholly to blame where he unforeseeably ran into the path of an oncoming moped: it was observed that on such facts it was preferable to regard the driver as without blame, as opposed to a finding that the pedestrian's behaviour amounted to a new intervening cause, eclipsing negligence of the driver). [For collision cases generally ...

Motor accidents

4–54 [*Add to line 1 of n.157 after "discussion"*]

... extended discussion] e.g. Ch.10, para.10-218, below. [Examples of contributory negligence ...

[*Add to n.158*]

A distinction between deliberate risk-taking by a pedestrian and simple misjudgement, was made in *Sabir v Osei-Kwabena* [2015] EWCA Civ 1213 (pedestrian who had misjudged the position of an approaching car, but had been clearly in view before being struck four metres into the road 25% to blame; driver 75%: the pedestrian had not put the motorist in danger or in an emergency situation: he ought reasonably to have seen her and taken his foot off the accelerator).

[*Add to n.159*]

... and see *Jackson v Murray* [2015] 2 All E.R. 805, SC, *per* Lord Reed at [39]-[43].

4–55 [*Add to text after n.165*]

There was no finding of contributory negligence where a motorcyclist had been travelling within the speed limit, even though it could be shown that if he had been travelling slower the accident could have been avoided.[165a]
NOTE 165a *Russell v National Farmers' Union Mutual Insurance Society Ltd* [2014] CSOH 157.

2.—AGREEMENT TO RUN THE RISK: "VOLENTI NON FIT INJURIA"

Contracting out of or limiting liability

4–85 [*Add to n.277*]

For changes to the Unfair Contract Terms Act 1977 on the coming into force of the Consumer Rights Act 2015 see Ch.2, para.2-214, n.482a, above. A Legislative Note summarising the effect of the new provisions appears in Appendix A to this Supplement.

Sport

4–100 [*Add to the end of n.336*]

... Rev 95]; Partington, "Professional liability of amateurs: the context of sports coaching" J.P.I. Law 2015, 4, 232.

Automatism, sudden illness or death

[Add to n.426 after the reference to Ryan v Youngs]   **4–135**

... 1 All E.R. 522.] The summary in the text was cited as a summary of the common law that applies to motor vehicle accidents in *Radice v Worster* [2015] EWHC 3732 (QB). The compatibility of a defence of automatism with European directives on liability in motor accident cases is left as an issue for trial.

4.—LIMITATION OF ACTION

(A) General Principles

Economic loss

[Add new paragraph to text]   **4–158a**

A distinction drawn, when considering the accrual of a cause of action in claims of professional negligence, between "no transaction" cases and "wrong transaction" cases, was considered by the Privy Council in *Maharaj v Johnson*.[505a] In giving the leading judgment Lord Wilson said that such a distinction was a helpful signpost towards the correct outcome rather than a determinative principle in its own right. It was essential to bear in mind that the central concept behind the two types of case was different. In the "wrong"—he preferred "flawed"—transaction case the claimant entered a flawed transaction in circumstances in which, in the absence of the defendant's breach of duty, he would have entered into an analogous, but flawless, transaction. In the "no transaction" case the claimant also entered into a transaction but in circumstances in which, in the absence of the defendant's breach of duty, he would have entered into "no transaction" at all. He went on[505b]:

> "The difference in concept dictates a difference in the inquiry as to whether, and if so when, the claimant suffered actual or measurable damage. In the "flawed transaction" case the inquiry is whether the value to the claimant of the flawed transaction was measurably less than what would have been the value to him of the flawless transaction. In the "no transaction" case the inquiry is whether, and if so at what point, the transaction into which the claimant entered caused his financial position to be measurably worse than if he had not entered into it ... "

Nykredit Mortgage Bank plc v Edward Erdman Group Ltd[505c] was an example of a "no transaction" case in that the claimants, who lent money on security of a property which valuers negligently overvalued for them, would otherwise have declined to make the loan.

NOTE 505a. [2015] UKPC 28 (an allegation that solicitors were negligent in failing to advise the claimants that a purported conveyance of land was ineffective to pass title to them since it was executed on behalf of someone who only held the land in the capacity of personal representative: when the claimants themselves attempted to sell the land many years later their questionable title was discovered and the transaction did not proceed).

NOTE 505b. See para.[19]. Observations in *Pegasus Management Holdings SCA v Ernst and Young* [2010] PNLR 438, CA and *Baker v Ollard and Bentley* 126 SJ 593, to the effect that if a transaction was flawed that of itself meant that the claimant suffered actual damage on entry into it, were criticised as going too far.
NOTE 505c. [1997] 1 WLR 1627, HL.

(B) Personal Injury litigation

Knowledge

4–188   *[Add to text after n.609]*

. . . inappropriate forceps.[609]] Where it was alleged that elders of a society of Jehovah's Witnesses had negligently failed to protect the claimant from sexual abuse at the hands of a minister to the society when she was a child, it was accepted she did not have actual knowledge of that failure until the exchange of witness statements in her assault claim.[609a]
NOTE 609a. *A v Trustees of the Watchtower Bible and Tract Society* [2015] EWHC 1722 (QB), Globe J, Ch.3, para.3-153, above.

Constructive knowledge

4–191   *[Add to n.615]*

It was reasonable to expect a person suffering from hearing loss to ask his specialist whether a history of noise exposure which they discussed had caused or contributed to his symptoms: *Platt v BRB (Residuary) Ltd* [2015] P.I.Q.R. P7, CA (had he done so, he would probably have been informed that his tinnitus and hearing loss were noise related and he thereby had constructive knowledge of the cause of his injury more than three years before a claim was commenced.

Importance of prejudice

4–208   *[Delete "646a" in line 5]*

All the circumstances of the case

4–215a   *[Add new paragraphs to text]*

Section 33(3) directs the court to consider "all the circumstances of the case" in addition to the factors specifically set out. The interplay between the two was considered in *Collins v Secretary of State for Business Innovation and Skills*,[706a] where it was observed that one relevant circumstance was pre-limitation delay, that is delay before a cause of action accrued to the claimant, and the existing authorities did not discuss its relevance at any great length. While the primary factors to consider were those set out in s.33(3)(a) to (f), pre-limitation period effluxion of time was also a relevant factor, although of less weight. Both parties could rely upon it for different purposes. A claimant might argue that it buttressed a case under s.33(3)(b); it may be said that recent delay had had little or no impact on the cogency of the evidence, the damage being done before any delay arose. The defendant could rely on the passage of time to show that it already faced massive difficulties in defending the action, and that any additional problems caused by the claimant's recent delay were therefore a serious matter. It was for the court to assess those and similar considerations before deciding on which side of the scales that factor should be placed.[706b]

In a noise induced deafness claim where it was accepted that the claimant had **4–215b** constructive knowledge sufficient to start the limitation clock ticking in 2001, but he continued in the same work thereafter for a period of three years and did not issue proceedings for a further ten, it was held that the exercise of discretion under s.33 should address two periods of time, before and after 2001. The three year period for injury sustained by 2001 expired in 2004 and there was prejudicial delay for five years after that before the claim was notified; likewise there was delay, albeit to a lesser extent, in relation to the injury sustained after 2001. All the circumstances had to be considered and care taken to give appropriate weight to pre limitation delay, also to delay after the claimant acquired knowledge, rather than focusing solely on the delay from the end of the limitation period. The Court of Appeal re-exercised the discretion and held it would be inequitable to allow the claim to proceed.[706c]

NOTE 706a. [2014] P.I.Q.R. P19, CA.

NOTE 706b. *Per* Jackson LJ at [66]. On the facts the trial judge had rightly declined to exercise discretion under s.33 where the claimant was guilty of some six years delay after acquiring constructive knowledge connecting his inoperable lung cancer to his exposure to asbestos between thirty and forty years earlier.

NOTE 706c. *Malone v Relyon Heating Engineering Ltd* [2014] EWCA Civ 904.

Walkley v Precision Forgings Ltd

[*n.719*]   **4–220**

Davidson v Aegis Defence Services (BVI) Ltd reported at [2014] 2 All E.R. 216, CA.

Limitation period not disapplied

[*Add to text at the end of the paragraph*]   **4–222**

The limitation period was not disapplied where the claimant alleged noise induced hearing loss against his former employer, a company which had been placed into liquidation over one year before he gave notice of his potential claim, where relevant personnel and occupational health records had been destroyed (in breach of normal document retention procedures) prior to the issue of proceeding, and no evidence could be procured from the company's former directors.[727a]

NOTE 727a. *Malone v Relyon Heating Engineering Ltd* [2014] EWCA Civ 904, para.4–215b, above.

Defendant company no longer in existence

4–225 *[Add to n.741]*

The discretion under s.1032(3) was considered in *Davy v Pickering* [2015] EWHC 380 (Ch).

(C) Latent Damage

Knowledge

4–230 *[Add to text after n.774]*

Where it was alleged that solicitors failed to advise the claimants that if they failed to file an objection to registration of a title to land by a certain date an adjudicator to HM Land Registry would have a statutory discretion whether or not to close the title, the "material fact about the damage" of which the claimants had to have knowledge for time to run under s.14A(6), was not the solicitors' failure to file an objection before the deadline, but that the effect of that failure was to allow a discretionary decision to be made against them in relation to the title.[774a]

NOTE 774a. *Blakemores LDP (In Administration) v Scott* [2015] EWCA Civ 999.

4–232 *[Add to n.779]*

. . . investigated as well.] See further *Schumann v Veale Wasbrough* [2015] EWCA Civ 441 (for purposes of an allegation of professional negligence against solicitors and a barrister who advised her not to proceed with a wrongful birth claim the claimant would have had constructive knowledge that the advice was wrong long before she consulted other lawyers; in any event the original advice had been correct); also *Capita ATL Pension Trustees Ltd v Sedgwick Financial Services Ltd* [2016] EWHC 214 (Ch) (in a claim by pension trustees against their financial advisors s.14(10) would only apply when the relevant fact could only be discovered with expert assistance. In the instant case non experts could have identified the relevant fact, so s.14(10) did not assist the claimants.)

[Add to text after n.780]

. . . had not read it.780] Also, for purposes of a claim against a financial advisor who allegedly gave negligent advice to the claimant to invest in an investment bond, time ran from the date when she might reasonably have been expected to learn that she had suffered damage in that return of the amount invested was not guaranteed.[780a] Mere uncertainty about the quantification of a loss does not mean that the claimant can take advantage of section 14A.[780b] [It is not reasonable . . .

NOTE 780a. *Jacobs v Sesame Ltd.* [2015] P.N.L.R. 6, CA (Tomlinson LJ referred at [27] to the important guidance given in relation to s.14A (10) by Arden LJ in *Gravgaard v Aldridge & Brownlee*, n.779, above).

NOTE 780b. *Toombs v Bridging Loans Ltd* [2014] EWHC 4566 (QB).

(D) Miscellaneous Limitation Periods

Periods of limitation prescribed by other Acts

[Add to n.792] **4–237**

Neither a consent order after a claimant accepted a defendant's Pt.36 offer, or a later costs order, constituted a "judgment" in a personal injury claim by which the defendant was held liable to the claimant for his injuries, and therefore did not fall within s.10(3) of the 1980 Act: *Chief Constable of Hampshire v Southampton City Council* [2015] P.I.Q.R. P5, CA.

[Add to n.296] **4–238**

See *Feest v South West SHA* [2014] 1 Lloyd's Rep. 419 where, in considering the limitation period of two years under arts.14 and 16 of the Athens Convention of 1974, the court drew attention to the words of Lord Macmillan in *Stag Line v Foscolo Mango & Co Ltd* [1932] A.C. 328 that in construing the Hague rules "their interpretation should not be rigidly controlled by precedents of antecedent date, but rather . . . should be construed on broad principles of general acceptation."

5.—OTHER DEFENCES

(A) Henderson v Henderson

Nature of the test

[Add to n.838] **4–250**

See also *Ridgewood Properties Group Ltd v Kilpatrick Stockton LLP* [2014] P.N.L.R. 31 (the administration of justice would be brought into disrepute if the claimants were permitted to re-litigate against a different party, issues decided against them in an earlier judgment which they had not appealed).

Irrelevant factors

[Add to n.842] **4–253**

. . . against a tortfeasor)]; also *Ridgewood Properties Group Ltd v Kilpatrick Stockton LLP* [2014] P.N.L.R. 31 (it would bring the administration of justice into disrepute to permit the claimant to seek as damages against its former legal advisors, loss which it had failed to recover in an earlier action against different parties where it wished essentially to challenge the factual findings in the earlier proceedings.

Merger and res judicata

[Note 845] **4–254**

Clark v In Focus Asset Management & Tax Solutions Ltd reported at [2014] P.N.L.R. 19, CA.

CHAPTER 4

(B) Illegality

Generally

4–258 *[Add new footnote reference 853a to "principles" in the last line]*

NOTE 853a. The nature of the act required to engage the *ex turpi causa* defence was considered in *Les Laboratoires Servier v Apotex Inc* [2015] A.C. 430. See particularly Lord Sumption JSC at [23] onwards: whether an act was of a quality to engage the defence depended upon its legal character; criminal acts were sufficient, but also quasi criminal acts, that is, other wrongful acts which engaged the public interest. Quasi criminal acts included "cases of dishonesty or corruption, which have always been regarded as engaging the public interest even in the context of purely civil disputes; some anomalous categories of misconduct, such as prostitution, which without itself being criminal are contrary to public policy and involve criminal liability on the part of secondary parties; and the infringement of statutory rules enacted for the protection of the public interest and attracting civil sanctions of a penal character, such as the competition law . . . "

Gray v Thames Trains Ltd

4–259 *[Add to n.855]*

. . . 159 N.L.J. 1200]; Goudkamp and Zou, "The defence of illegality in tort law: beyond judicial redemption?" 2015 C.L.J. 74(1) 13. [*Gray* was applied . . .

The wider rule

4–261 *[Add to n.864]*

The *ex turpi causa* rule defeated claims by two passengers who jumped from a moving taxi in order to avoid paying the fare: *Beaumont v Ferrer* [2015] P.I.Q.R. P2, Ch.6, para.6-92, below. In applying the rule Kenneth Parker J was not persuaded that proportionality (as between the claimant's misconduct and the result if he were denied a remedy) had a part to play: "[38] . . . There is considerable doubt whether the Court should seek to weigh the degree and culpability of the claimant's criminality against the conduct of the defendant, and to allow a remedy if the Court concluded that the defendant's conduct was by far the more culpable. *Clerk and Lindsell on Torts* (20th edn. 2010) at 3–37 sets out powerful objections to the incorporation of "proportionality" in the relevant sense in the public policy underpinned by *ex turpi causa*, and it appears to me that the recent case of *Joyce v O'Brien* [2012] EWHC 1324 (QB); [20131 EWCA Civ 546 tends to support the proposition that 'proportionality' has ordinarily no role to play." See further, *Tavares*, "*Beaumont v Ferrer: personal injury—road traffic accidents*" J.P.I. Law 2014, 4, C211.

[Add to the end of n.867]

See also *McCracken v Smith* [2015] EWCA Civ 380. Where two 16-year-old boys rode a trials motorbike designed only for one rider, neither wore a crash hat and it was driven too fast down a cycle path into collision with a minibus, the ex turpi principle was applied so as to prevent the boy who was a passenger suing the driver of the bike for his injuries. He could, however, recover against the driver of the minibus who had himself been negligent in failing to keep a proper look-out. The conduct which gave rise to the ex turpi defence was one of two causes of the collision, the minibus driver's negligence being the other. The correct approach was to give effect to both causes by allowing the passenger to claim in negligence against the driver of the minibus but to reduce any damages for contributory negligence. The correct deduction was 65% of which 15% reflected the failure to wear a helmet. See further, *Smith v Stratton* [2015] EWCA Civ 1413.

Stone & Rolls Ltd v Moore Stephens

[Add to n.871]   **4–263**

In *Jetivia SA v Bilta (UK) Ltd* [2015] 2 W.L.R. 1168 SC, Lord Neuberger stated *obiter* at [30] that *Stone & Rolls* should be put to one side as "it is not in the interests of the future clarity of the law for it to be treated as authoritative or of assistance." *Jetivia* was concerned with the attribution to a company of illegal conduct by a director in the context of a claim against that director. The Court held that attribution was inappropriate in such a case, and therefore the company's claim would not be barred. Lord Neuberger, with whom on this point the other justices agreed, considered that *Stone & Rolls* should only be seen as standing for two propositions; first that an illegality defence cannot be run against a company by a third party where the directing mind and will acted fraudulently in circumstances where the company has innocent shareholders or directors; second, that the defence would be available where knowledge could be attributed to a "one-man company," who would not have innocent shareholders or directors. However, there was less agreement about what else, if anything *Stone & Rolls* should be seen as standing for. It seems clear that the case will have to be revisited by the Supreme Court (see e.g. Lord Sumption at para.[81]).

Such future reconsideration may take place alongside a detailed consideration of the basis for the illegality defence, where the justices in *Jetivia* were split between Lord Sumption, who held that a defence would arise automatically whenever the claimant engaged in illegal activity; and Lords Hodge and Toulson, who held that a judge would have to make an assessment of all the circumstances of the illegal activity before deciding whether a defence arises. Lord Sumption relied upon his judgement in *Les Laboratories Servier v Apotex* [2015] AC 430, whereas Lords Hodge and Toulson drew on the judgment of Lord Wilson in *Hounga v Allen* [2014] 1 WLR 2889, SC. These two judgements provide conflicting accounts of the law relating to illegality, and there is no doubt clarification is required.

Deliberate exaggeration

[Add to n.875]   **4–265**

... fraudulent claims.] Nevertheless Parliament responded with s.57 of the Criminal Justice and Courts Act 2015, which comes into force on a day to be appointed and provides a number of sanctions, including dismissal of the claim, if someone claiming damages for personal injury is found to have been "fundamentally dishonest" in relation to the claim or a related claim. See Spencer and Kinley, "The truth hurts" N.L.J. 2015, (7638), 11; Chambers, "Fundamental injustice?" 2015 S.J. 159, 18.

(D) Striking out negligence claims

Factual allegations to be assumed

4–267   [*Add to text after n.880*]

... should the claim be dismissed.[880]] It is not appropriate on a summary judgment hearing to engage in a close examination of the witness statements and pleadings with the object of rejecting selected parts of the evidence without the opportunity of cross examination.[880a] [The drawbacks ...

NOTE 880a. *Blakemores LDP (In Administration) v Scott* [2015] EWCA Civ 999, para.4-230, above, *per* Vos LJ at [42]. It is, however, perfectly in order to reject witness statements where they are plainly contradicted by unchallenged contemporaneous documents.

CHAPTER 5

PROOF AND DAMAGES

1.—Remoteness of Damage

(B) Proof by inference

Facts more consistent with negligence than other causes

[Add to text after n.50]   **5–10**

There is no principle in clinical negligence cases, analogous to the admissibility of bad character evidence in criminal law, by which the court can infer negligence in performing one operation from evidence of incompetence in performing others. Evidence of extraneous matters should be confined to cases within the "similar fact" principle for the traditional reason that, unless it was similar fact evidence, it was not probative of the issue to be determined.[50a]

Note 50a. *Laughton v Shalaby* [2015] P.I.Q.R. P6, CA (an allegation of negligence against a surgeon who performed a hip replacement operation, it having been found by the General Medical Council that his treatment of certain other patients fell below the expected standard. The CA opined that evidence of lack of probity would be relevant to the credibility of a witness, but it was the surgeon's competence that was in issue, not his credibility. The most that could be said was that any lack of probity proved could show that he would be unlikely to admit to any incompetence or that he was less likely to have followed his standard practice than he asserted. That was a slender basis on which to advance a negligence case. Moreover, on the facts, the examples of his lack of probity were not of the most serious kind. The claimant could not rely on general adverse comment in the GMC report unless she could point to other cases which could constitute similar fact evidence. On the facts, that was impossible: knee, foot and wrist operations were too far removed from hip operations to constitute such evidence. The only other hip replacement considered in the report had been criticised for insufficient discussion with the patient, which could also not be considered similar fact (see judgment at [21]-[26]).

CHAPTER 5

(D) Proof and Causation

Generally

5–46 [*Add to n.180*]

... P324, CA], n.175, above. An adverse inference was not drawn when, on the trial of a clinical negligence claim, the defendant failed to call a doctor who had explained the procedure to her on the day of the operation and who had attended the operation. *Wiszniewski*, above, was distinguished the absent witness in that case having been the doctor whose negligence was said to have caused the harm. In the instant case, the absent doctor's position had been far more tangential: See *Manzi v King's College Hospital NHS Foundation Trust* [2016] EWHC 1101 (QB).

5–47 [*Add to text at the end of the paragraph*]

It was a false premise for a judge, in deciding the cause of a house fire, to conclude that if it was not arson it had on a balance of probability to be the negligence of a neighbour: the ultimate question was whether the court was satisfied that the suggested explanation was more likely than not to be true, and the approach taken did not allow for the position that the claimant had simply failed to prove the cause.[176a]

NOTE 176a. *Graves v Brouwer* [2015] EWCA Civ 595 (about 30 minutes before fire broke out in the roof space of the claimant's house her neighbour set fire some card and paper in a narrow alley which separated the two properties and experts' disagreed whether that fire could have been responsible for later fire).

Applying the balance of probability test

5–48 [*Add to n.187*]

; also *Love v Halfords Ltd* [2014] P.I.Q.R. P20 (another bicycle accident).

2.—DAMAGES GENERALLY

General principles

5–53 [*Add new footnote 204a to "negligence" in line 17*]

NOTE 204a. If the defendant could have discharged its duty in more than one way, it is entitled, on the assessment of damages, to ask the court to suppose it would have adopted the method most favourable to itself, i.e. that which produces the lower measure of damages: *Agouman v Leigh Day* [2016] EWHC 1324 (QB), [130], Andrew Smith J.

[*Add to text at the end of the paragraph*]

There is a principle of proportionality in the calculation of damages, and it is legitimate to consider whether a benefit that is intended to be achieved by a particular item of expenditure can be achieved by cheaper means. Never-theless, in cases where there is no alternative way to provide the claimant with proper compensation, recovery of the cost of an item of damage will not be refused on the grounds that it is disproportionate to the benefit the claimant will receive.[208a]

Mitigation of damage

[*Add new footnote reference 213a to "concerned" in line 11 on page* [387]]

5–54

NOTE 213a. See e.g. *Bacciottini v Gotelee & Goldsmith* [2016] EWCA Civ 170 (only nominal damages recovered where solicitors had negligently failed to identify a planning restriction on a conveyance of land, but the claimants had successfully made an application to remove it, and the value of the land was not affected. It was observed that the assessment of damages was to be undertaken realistically and not mechanistically; the factual context was critically important to the determination of the proper measure of damages to be applied and the need to secure a fair outcome.

3.—HEADS OF DAMAGES AND THEIR ASSESSMENT

(B) Damage to chattels, land and buildings

Generally

[*Add to n.277*]

5–71

The usual rule, that is that the recoverable loss for damage to a chattel is the diminution in its value on the date damage occurred, was applied in *Waterdance Ltd v Kingston Marine Services Ltd* [2014] B.L.R. 141. The chattel in question was a fishing vessel which suffered damage to her engine requiring repairs estimated in the sum of £435,000. The repairs were not in fact carried out because several months after the relevant incident the claimant decommissioned the vessel thereby receiving in excess of £1m under a government scheme. The defendant's case that no damage had been suffered was rejected. It had failed to establish that no diminution in value occurred as at the date damage occurred. What if anything the claimant would recover under the scheme was uncertain at that stage. On the facts the vessel had been worth in excess of the sum eventually received under the scheme and the prima facie measure of damages was the cost of repairs.

[*Note 279*]

Coles v Hetherton reported at [2015] 1 W.L.R. 160, CA

[*Add to n.279*]

... Civ 1704] (the basic loss was the diminution in value of the damaged vehicle as evidenced by the cost of reasonable repair; by whatever mechanism the car was repaired the claimant's loss was to be judged by the reasonable-ness of the overall sum paid for repair as compared with the reasonable cost of repair on the open market). See *Fairhurst*, "Vehicular diminution" N.L.J. 2015, 165(7637), 12.

Credit car hire

5–76   *[Add to n.302]*

See *Stevens v Equity Syndicate Management Ltd* [2015] R.T.R. 24, CA (the ideal way to calculate the fair and reasonable cost of credit hire, excluding any irrecoverable element of the charge in fact made by the credit hire company, is to take the lowest reasonable rate that would have been charged to the claimant by a mainstream supplier for a car of the type in question).

(C) Damages for personal injuries

Loss of congenial employment

5–104   *[Add to the start of n.397]*

For an award where the claimant had served in the armed forces, see *Murphy v Ministry of Defence* [2016] EWHC 3 (QB). [There is a table . . .

Actual and prospective loss

5–109   *[Note 412]*

Haxton v Philips Electronics UK Ltd reported at [2014] P.I.Q.R. P11, CA.

5–110   *[Add new footnote reference 418a to "genuine" in line 9 on page [411]]*

NOTE 418a. Where the claimant's loss includes an expense incurred, for example, by the purchase of goods or services, it is not necessary to prove that the price paid was the cheapest available. Provided the claimant acts reasonably, as where there is a real difference between what is purchased and any alternative goods or services available at a lower price, the higher-priced items will be recoverable: *Miller v Imperial College Healthcare NHS Trust* [2014] EWHC 3772 (QB) [100]-[101]).

Gratuitously provided care and assistance

5–117   *[Add to n.437]*

See also *Finnie v South Devon Healthcare NHS Foundation Trust* [2014] EWHC 4333 (QB), *per* Dingemans J. at [43].

(iii) *Future pecuniary loss*

Generally

5–125a   *[Add new paragraph to text]*

An issue has arisen whether, when considering compensation for the reasonable future needs of the claimant, arising from a negligently inflicted disability, and there are a range of reasonable options, the cheapest should be selected.[469a] It has been suggested that there should be proportionality between the cost of an item and the benefit the claimant will derive from it.[469b] In determining whether a claimant's reasonable needs require that a given item of expenditure should be incurred, "the court must consider whether the same or a substantially similar result could be achieved by other, less expensive, means".[469c] The basic and underlying principle however, of which proportionality is simply an element, is reasonableness.[469d] The focus is upon the claimant's needs and not, for instance, the provision of pleasure, unless that is incidental to some identifiable therapeutic benefit.[469e]

A difficulty can also arise in assessing future pecuniary loss where, at the time **5–125b** the claimant's injury was sustained, he or she was already suffering a degree of disability which would have caused similar loss in any event. Such was the case where the claimant was being treated in hospital for an inflammatory condition which damaged her spinal cord and led to her being classified as T7 paraplegic. That injury was not tortiously inflicted but during her hospital stay, as a result of negligence in treatment, she suffered pressure sores which caused osteomyelitis, spasms and associated deep infection. On the assessment of damages it was argued on behalf of the defendant that in money terms she was no worse off than she would have been in any event as a result of her paraplegia. That submission was rejected by the Court of Appeal. Where the claimant condition was made quantitatively, but not qualitatively, worse by the negligence, then only the additional cost would compensated. Where the needs were made qualitatively worse, then the defendant would be liable for the entirety of those needs.[469f]

NOTE 469a. The issue was set out by Foskett J. in his judgment in *Robshaw v United Lincolnshire Hospitals NHS Trust* [2015] EWHC 923 (QB) at [162].

NOTE 469b. *Whiten v St. George's* [2011] EWHC 2066 (QB) *per* Swift J. at [5].

NOTE 469c. *Per* Warby J. in *Ellison v University Hospitals of Morecambe Bay NHS Foundation Trust* [2015] EWHC 366 (QB) at [18].

NOTE 469d. *Robshaw v United Lincolnshire Hospitals NHS Trust*, above, at [166].

NOTE 469e. See para.[290], allowing the cost of a home-based swimming pool in a claim of brain injury; also *per* Swift J. in *Whiten*, above, at [262], disallowing claims for aquatic physiotherapy. See also *HS v Lancashire Teaching Hospitals NHS Trust* [2015] EWHC 1376 (QB) (claim for a hydrotherapy pool in the family home of a severely injured claimant not allowed).

NOTE 469f. *Reaney v University Hospital of Staffordshire NHS Trust* [2015] EWCA Civ 1119; [2016] P.I.Q.R. Q3, CA, following *Performance Cars v Abraham* [1962] 1 Q.B. 33, *Baker v Willoughby* [1970] A.C. 467 and *Halsey v Milton Keynes General NHS Trust* [2004] 1 W.L.R. 3002, CA.

Private care and publicly funded care

[*Add to n.475*] **5–127**

See also *Harman v East Kent Hospitals NHS Foundation Trust* [2015] P.I.Q.R. Q4 (where the parents of a severely handicapped child, already receiving care in a residential home funded by the local authority, expressed a firm and genuine desire that such care be funded by the defendant Trust, damages were assessed accordingly: there was no requirement that the court adjudicate on the question whether their preference was reasonable).

The Ogden Tables

5–133   [*Add to n.486*]

... how should it be set".] In *LHS v First-Tier Tribunal* [2015] P.I.Q.R. Q2 the court rejected the argument that the 2.5% discount rate should not be applied in a claim before the Criminal Injuries Compensation Authority: see Ch.17, para.17-38, below.

[*Add footnote reference 488a to "disability" in line 13*]

NOTE 488a. See Regan, "The Ogden conundrum" N.L.J. 2014, 164 (7630), 10 (considers *Billett v Ministry of Defence*, below, and the perceived need to depart from the Ogden formula to avoid over-compensation).

Adjustments to the multiplier

5–134   [*Add new footnote reference 489a to "cases" in the first line*]

NOTE 489a. The difficulties that can arise in applying the Ogden Tables are illustrated in *Billett v Ministry of Defence* [2014] EWHC 3060 (QB). The trial judge, Andrew Edis QC, was required to consider the effect of a relatively minor non freezing cold injury upon the claimant's future earnings capacity. He rejected the Blamire approach (for which see para.5-136, below) on the basis that the claimant's future working pattern was not so uncertain as to justify it. However in applying the Ogden Tables on the basis that the claimant was "disabled" he drew attention to the risk of over compensation given the relatively moderate injury the claimant had suffered. He went on, at [61]:

> "my multiplier will be substantially reduced for contingencies other than mortality to reflect the minor nature of the disability. I consider that in the absence of any other evidence or guidance I should take a mid-point between the not disabled RF (reduction factor) of 0.92 and the disabled RF of 0.54, which is 0.73. There is little logic in this approach, except that it gives a figure which appears to me to reflect fully the loss sustained by the Claimant, but to do so in a way which does not obviously overstate that loss. A judicial approach to the assessment of damages involves an exercise of judgment in the individual case being considered. Sometimes statistics give an answer which appears obviously too high, given the picture which emerges in the particular case. Where that happens, the Judge has to make an apparently arbitrary adjustment to that result, or to decline to use the statistical material at all".

See further, Cottrell, "Future imperfect" 2015 J.P.I.L. (1), 42.

Loss of career prospects

5–138   [*Add to the end of n.497*]

... Q13, CA] In *Tate v Ryder Holdings* [2014] EWHC 4256 (QB) Kenneth Parker J refused to reduce damages on the basis that the claimant, who was injured when he was eleven, would have lived a life of irregular employment and substance abuse, observing, at [33], it is "extraordinarily difficult in any event to evaluate in any acceptable or convincing way how this particular Claimant, aged only 11 at the time that he sustained this devastating organic brain injury, would have developed" and such speculation "could be quite wrong and seriously unfair . . . "

Lost years claims

[*Add to n.510*]   **5–142**

The views expressed in *Iqbal* were repeated in *Totham v King's College Hospital NHS Foundation Trust* [2015] Med. L.R. 55, Elisabeth Laing J.

CHAPTER 6

CAUSATION AND REMOTENESS OF DAMAGE

2.—CAUSE IN FACT

(A) "But for" causation

Over-exclusionary operation

6–10   [*Add to n.20*]

See also, Steel, "Justifying exceptions to proof of causation in tort law" M.L.R. 2015, 78(5), 729.

The counterfactual question

6–10a   [*Add new paragraph to text*]

Application of the "but for" test inevitably involves a counterfactual question, that is, what would have happened, so far as the claimant's loss is concerned, had the defendant complied with the relevant duty of care. The complications that can arise where the duty could have been complied with in a number of different ways, some of which would have avoided that loss, some not, were examined in *Robbins v Bexley LBC*,[20a] a claim based on damage to a house from the roots of trees located in a park the defendant local authority was obliged to maintain. Nothing was done by the authority to avoid such damage after a time when it became foreseeable. The judge at first instance found that a reasonable system would have involved a cyclical reduction in the crowns of the trees by 25%, but that such work would itself have been insufficient to avoid the damage. The claimant nonetheless succeeded, on a finding that in carrying the system into effect the defendant's contractors would have gone further than strictly required and carried out more extensive reduction work, which would have been sufficient to prevent the damage. In effect, the claimant could rely upon a counterfactual finding that the defendant would actually have behaved in a more generous way than the standard of reasonable care minimally required.

NOTE 20a. [2014] B.L.R. 11, CA. For a discussion of the implications of the decision, see Steel, "Defining causal counterfactuals in negligence" (2014) LQR 564. The editor shares the author's concerns about the consistency of this decision with principle.

Bonnington Castings Ltd. v Wardlaw

[*Add to n.29*]   **6–13**

... at 621.] In *Chetwynd v Tunmore* [2016] EWHC 156 (QB) *Bonnington Castings* was not regarded as applicable to a case where a series of fishing lakes on the claimant's land suffered from reduced water levels following the excavation of four new lakes on the defendant's land. HHJ Reddihough (sitting as a judge of the High Court) held, at [33], that the "material contribution" test could not properly be extended to such a case and the usual "but for" causation test should be applied.

[*Add to n.30*]   **6–14**

... infliction of the injury]. A similar view of the effect of *Bonnington Castings* seems to have been adopted by the Privy Council in *Williams v Bermuda Hospitals Board* [2016] UKPC 4; [2016] 2 W.L.R. 774, SC.

[*Add new footnote reference 30a to "rule" in line 7*]

NOTE 30a. See *per* Lord Dyson MR in *Heneghan v Manchester Dry Docks Ltd* [2016] EWCA Civ 86 at [23] where he said:

> "There are three ways of establishing causation in disease cases. The first is by showing that but for the defendant's negligence, the claimant would not have suffered the disease. Secondly, where the disease is caused by the cumulative effect of an agency part of which is attributable to breach of duty on the part of the defendant and part of which involves no breach of duty, the defendant will be liable on the ground that his breach of duty made a "material contribution" to the disease: *Bonnington Castings Ltd v Wardlaw* [1956] AC 613. The disease in that case was pneumoconiosis which is a divisible disease (i.e. one whose severity increases with increased exposure to the agency). Thirdly, where causation cannot be proved in either of these ways, for example because the disease is indivisible, causation may be established if it is proved that the defendant materially increased the risk of the victim contracting the disease: the Fairchild exception. Mesothelioma is an indivisible disease."

[*Add to n.33*]

The statement of the Court of Appeal in *Bailey* that the decision involved a departure from the "but-for" test was said to be wrong by the Privy Council in *Williams v Bermuda Health Board* , n. 30, above at [47] "The Board does not share the view of the Court of Appeal that the case involved a departure from the "but-for" test. The judge concluded that the totality of the claimant's weakened condition caused the harm. If so, "but-for" causation was established. The fact that her vulnerability was heightened by her pancreatitis no more assisted the hospital's case than if she had an egg shell skull." For criticism of both the "but for" and "material contribution" tests see Turton, "Using NESS to overcome the confusion created by the 'material contribution to harm' test for causation in negligence" (2014) 2 PN 50.

Bonnington and consecutive causes

[*Add new paragraph to text*]   **6–14a**

The Privy Council applied *Bonnington Castings* to consecutive causes in *Williams v Bermuda Hospitals Board*.[33a] The claimant had suffered injury to his heart and lungs as a result of sepsis resulting from appendicitis. The sepsis developed incrementally over a six hour period between hospital admission and surgery. Part of this time was a negligent delay. The non-negligent and negligent periods of time operated as consecutive and cumulative causes of the totality of the sepsis. Each period had made a material contribution to the totality of the septic process, and therefore, on the balance of probabilities the delay had made a material contribution to the injury to the heart and lungs, The Privy Council made clear that *Bonnington Castings* applies where the cumulative causes are consecutive, as well as when they are concurrent. In *John v Central Manchester and Manchester Children's University Hospitals NHS Foundation Trust*[33b] the principle was extended further to multiple factor consecutive cases. Where one factor, amongst many consecutive factors made a material contribution to the totality of the injury it can be regarded as a cause in law of the injury. So, on the facts in *John* a negligent delay in treatment made a material contribution to the totality of the cognitive and neurophysiological injury suffered by the claimant in a case where it was the second in a series of three matters that contributed to the damage. The claimant had non-negligently fallen down stairs, suffered a negligent delay in treatment and a non-negligent post-operative infection, all of which led to raised inter-cranial pressure. Taken together, the sequence of events led to the eventual outcome and therefore each event had made a material contribution to the injury.

Note 33a. *Williams v Bermuda Hospitals Board*, n.30, above.

Note 33b. [2016] EWHC 407 (QB); [2016] 4 W.L.R. 54.

Apportionment in exposure cases

6–15   [*Add to text after n.34*]

... at particular times.[34] Where apportionment between tortious and non-tortious factors is impossible then the tortfeasor will be liable for the entire extent of the injury, notwithstanding that it is accepted that the tortious factor did not contribute to 100% of the damage.[34a]

Note 34a. *John v Central Manchester and Manchester Children's University Hospitals NHS Foundation Trust*, n.33b, above.

(B) Proof of risk of harm

Creation of risk and proof of breach

6–31a   [*Add new paragraph*]

Fairchild did not assist claimants in a group action who alleged that smoke and fumes from a fire on premises for which the defendant was responsible had materially increased the risk to them of injury, albeit the evidence that they had in fact suffered injury was weak and implausible. In order to prove that the risk of injury had been materially increased an individual claimant had to establish exposure to noxious agents at a level which was capable of causing personal injury. The evidence fell far short of establishing that proposition to the requisite standard.[58a]

Note 58a. *Saunderson v Sonae Industria (UK) Ltd* [2015] EWHC 2264, Jay J.

Compensation Act 2006, s.3

[Add new note 62a to "liability" in the last line] **6–36**

NOTE 62a In *Zurich Insurance plc v International Energy Group Limited* [2015] UKSC 33 the Supreme Court confirmed that proportionate liability will continue to apply in *Fairchild* cases beyond the scope of the 2006 Act. Proportionate liability was appropriate where the claimant suffered lung cancer as a result of exposure to asbestos where the *Fairchild* exception applied: see *Heneghan v Manchester Dry Docks Ltd*, n.30a, above. See also, *Morgan "Reinterpreting the reinterpretation of the reinterpretation of Fairchild"* C.L.J. 2015, 74(3), 395.

Insurance implications

6–41a

[Add new paragraph]

In *Zurich Insurance plc v International Energy Group Limited*[68a] the Supreme Court considered whether employers' liability insurers were liable to cover the entirety of insured's loss resulting from liability in damages and costs for negligent exposure to asbestos which resulted in mesothelioma, where causation was demonstrated on a *Fairchild* basis. Where the Compensation Act 2006 does not apply the insurer is only liable for a proportionate share of the damages calculated by reference to the proportion of the negligent exposure for which the insurer was on cover. However, the insurer is liable for 100% of the insured's legal costs. Where the Act does apply the insurer is liable for 100% of the insured's damages and costs, subject to equitable rights to contribution from any other EL insurer on cover during the employee's period of employment, or from the insured where there are periods of self-insurance during the employee's period of employment. The nature and extent of these equitable rights are outside the scope of this work.
NOTE 68a. [2015] 2 W.L.R. 1471, SC.

Appraisal

[Add to n.70] **6–42**

Fairchild was applied to a lung cancer case in *Heneghan v Manchester Dry Docks Ltd* [2016] EWCA Civ 86. The claimant's attempt to establish liability for the full amount of loss against any of six defendants, each of whom was responsible for a culpable exposure of less than 50%, failed. The argument that responsibility for a material increase in the risk of the claimant developing lung cancer, was treated in law as causing the disease itself was rejected.

Per Lord Dyson MR: there is a fundamental difference between making a material contribution to an injury and materially increasing the risk of an injury. The decision in *Fairchild* had not been based on the fiction that a defendant who had created a material risk of mesothelioma was deemed to have caused or materially contributed to the contraction of the disease. The "material contribution test" set out in *Bonnington Castings v Wardlaw* applied in cases where the court was satisfied on scientific evidence that the exposure for which the defendant was responsible had, in fact, contributed to the injury.

That was readily demonstrated in the case of divisible injuries, the severity of which was proportionate to the amount of exposure to the causative agent. However, where the scientific evidence did not permit a finding that the exposure attributable to a particular defendant contributed to the injury, the *Fairchild* exception applied. In the instant case, the evidence permitted the contribution to the risk of cancer attributable to an individual respondent to be quantified, but it went no further than that. It was not possible to infer that all or any of the respondents had made a material contribution to lung cancer being contracted. However, all of them had materially contributed to the risk that the disease would be contracted. In the event that *Fairchild* was applied the parties agreed that the damages should be apportioned pursuant to the approach in *Barker v Corus (UK) Ltd.*, n.60, above. See further Steel, "On when Fairchild applies" L.Q.R. 2015, 131(Jul), 363; Allen, "The extension of Fairchild to lung cancer" J.P.I. Law 2016, 2, 61.

See also the statement of Lord Hodge in *Zurich Insurance plc v International Energy Group Limited* [2015] UKSC 33 at [98] that "th[e] innovative rule of causation [in *Fairchild*] . . . is not confined to mesothelioma." Also *per* Lords Neuberger and Reed in the same case at [191]: the Fairchild exception is "applicable to any disease which has the unusual features of mesothelioma." It does not appear that the dicta of Baroness Hale in *Re J (Children)* [2013] 1 A.C. 680 at [41] that the "exception applies only where the claimant has contracted mesothelioma . . . a special rule, created only because of the special difficulty of proving causation in mesothelioma cases" was cited to either court, and that observation must now be regarded as incorrect.

Continuing role for a "doubles the risk" test?

6–45a *[Add new paragraph to text]*

The decision of the Court of Appeal in *Heneghan v Manchester Dry Docks Ltd*[74a] illustrates an important continuing use for the doubling of risk principle. In a case where there are competing possible mechanisms causing a loss (in *Heneghan* asbestos and smoking) it is appropriate to use doubling the risk to determine which mechanism caused the injury. Lord Dyson MR observed that the doubling of risk test can be useful to enable courts to determine "what" was responsible for the injury to the claimant, even if it was not useful to determine "who" was responsible when multiple employers had exposed the claimant to asbestos. In *Heneghan*, it was shown that the risk of cancer from asbestos was more than double the risk of lung cancer from smoking. Therefore the smoking could be disregarded as a cause of the lung cancer. Once the "what" had been determined, the *Fairchild/Barker* exception could be applied to hold that each employer would be liable to the claimant on the basis that they had materially increased the risk, removing the challenge of the approach in *Wilsher v Essex Area Health Authority*[74b] which appears to remain good law for the proposition that material increase in the risk is not sufficient to demonstrate causation where there are multiple possible causal agents.

NOTE 74a. [2016] EWCA Civ 86, n.70, above.
NOTE 74b. Above para.6-22.

Conclusion

[Add to the end of n.76]　　　　　　　　　　　　　　　　　**6–48**

... p.68]. See similar views expressed in *Zurich Insurance plc v International Energy Group Limited* [2015] UKSC 33, above (e.g. Lords Neuberger and Reed at [191]).

(D) Loss of a chance

Loss of a chance

[Add to the end of n.86]　　　　　　　　　　　　　　　　　**6–54**

A similar approach has been applied to a dependency claim under the Fatal Accidents Act 1976: see *Hayes v South East Coast Ambulance Service NHS Foundation Trust* [2015] EWHC 18 (QB), Ch.16, para.16-42, below.

(B) Intervening third party conduct

Deliberate Acts

[Add to text at the end of the paragraph]　　　　　　　　　　**6–84**

... overseas.[153] A fraudulent claim, upheld by a corrupt judiciary, cannot break the chain of causation between a breach by a solicitor of a duty to protect settlement monies from dishonest claims and corrupt judicial decisions, and the loss suffered by the claimants for whom the monies were held.[153a]

NOTE 153a. *Agouman v Leigh Day* [2016] EWHC 1324 (QB), [120], Andrew Smith J.

3.—CAUSE IN LAW

(C) Intervening act of claimant

Intervening cause

[Add to text at the end of the paragraph]　　　　　　　　　　**6–92**

Even if a taxi driver, who drove off after realising that two passengers intended to leave the taxi without paying, was at fault, he was not liable to them in negligence where it was their own action in jumping out of the moving vehicle which was held to be the cause of their injuries.[175a]

NOTE 175a. *Beaumont v Ferrer* [2015] P.I.Q.R. P2, Ch.4, para.4-261, above (six passengers planned to take the taxi without paying and three successfully ran off when it came to a halt; the driver then put the vehicle in motion in part to prevent the remaining passengers doing the same but two sustained injury when they jumped out).

CHAPTER 6

No intervening cause

6–93   [*Add to text at the end of the paragraph*]

There was no intervening cause where, following an minor road traffic accident, the claimant left his vehicle to inspect the damage, leaving his children inside, but failed to put the car in "park" and suffered crush injuries to his leg as he tried to prevent it rolling down a hill.[180a]

NOTE 180A. *Sparrow v Arnaud* [2016] EWHC 739 (QB).

4.—REMOTENESS OF DAMAGE

(C) Application of the foresight test

Scope of the relevant duty

6–144   [*Note 275*]

Haxton v Philips Electronics UK Ltd reported at [2014] P.I.Q.R. P11, CA.

THE STANDARD OF CARE

2.—MATTERS TO BE TAKEN INTO ACCOUNT

(C) Gravity of the consequences

Sporting activities

[Add to text after n.69] 7–28

A claim by a ball spotter at a golf tournament, who lost the sight of an eye after being struck by a competitor's ball, failed, on a finding that he had not been seen by the competitor before the ball was struck and in the circumstances his presence should not have been anticipated and it was reasonable for a warning not to be given.[69a]
NOTE 69a. *McMahon v Dear* [2014] CSOH 100.

(D) Cost and practicability

Importance of the end to be achieved

[Add to the end of n.80] 7–33

See further *Humphrey v Aegis Defence Services Ltd* [2016] EWCA Civ 11 (no breach of duty where the defendants included Iraqi interpreters, who did not have to reach the same standard of physical fitness as the claimant military contractor, in training exercises, despite this posing a foreseeable risk of injury due to the interpreters physical weakness. Moore-Bick LJ at [10] held that " . . . the scarcity of Iraqis willing to act as interpreters, the importance of their role and the need for them to work as part of a team with the contractors" could be taken into account in determining the standard of care. A reasonable person in the position of the defendant would not have been required either to restrict the recruitment of interpreters to those who reached the same level of fitness as the contractors or to stop interpreters taking part in training until they reached the necessary standard.)

Social Responsibility and Heroism Act 2015[83a]

[Add new paragraph to text] 7–34a

The need for this Act is not immediately clear and at this stage it would appear to complicate the task of identifying the conduct reasonably required of a

CHAPTER 7

defendant in discharging a duty of care, rather clarifying it. By s.1 the provisions are stated to apply when a court, "in considering a claim that a person was negligent or in breach of statutory duty, is determining the steps that the person was required to take to meet a standard of care." In considering the claim a court must have regard to each of three matters set out in ss.2 to 4: whether the alleged negligence or breach of statutory duty occurred when the person was acting for the benefit of society or any of its members; whether the person, in carrying out the activity in the course of which the alleged negligence or breach of statutory duty occurred, demonstrated a predominantly responsible approach towards protecting the safety or other interests of others; and whether the alleged negligence or breach of statutory duty occurred when the person was acting heroically[83b] by intervening in an emergency to assist an individual in danger. Each of these matters is a factor which, in an appropriate case, a court would already be expected to consider when deciding what standard of care was reasonably required of a defendant in the circumstances and to that extent the statute is unnecessary. There is a departure from the usual forensic process in the sense that the factors *must* be taken into account, so whether any party has actually asked that they be taken into account is irrelevant: the onus is placed on the court to consider them even if no-one else has.[83c] Finally, it is not said what "having regard" to a factor means in this context: no guidance is given about the weight that must be given to the factors in coming to a decision. It is not provided that they carry greater weight than, or exclude, any other consideration which might arise in deciding a particular case and had that been intended presumably Parliament would have so provided. In the result, having had regard to the factors, the court must do what it would have done anyway and decide what the defendant's duty of care reasonably required of him.

NOTE 83a. 2015 c. 3. The main provisions of the Act will come into force on a day to be appointed.

NOTE 83b. "Heroically" is not defined, presumably on the basis that heroism is self-evident, although there may be circumstances where what appears heroic to one person is regarded as recklessly undertaking an unreasonable risk by another. See further Ch.2, para.2-272, and Ch.4, 4-115, above in relation to "rescuers". And if D, in heroically trying to save A from harm, owes a duty of care to C, of which he is on the face of it in breach, why should his heroism towards A have any effect on the outcome of C's claim?

NOTE 83c. On usual principles, if by any chance, a party does not raise the matters set out in the Act it will be the duty of the court to give the opportunity for evidence to be led and submissions made in relation to them since they will have to form some part of the decision. Before a trial consideration will have to be given to the evidence required to support the proposition that the defendant was acting for the benefit of society or its members; or whether in carrying out the activity the defendant was demonstrating a predominantly responsible approach to safety or "other interests", whatever they may be. And what does "predominantly" add? May there be cases where a defendant was acting responsibly to an extent, but not predominantly?

CHAPTER 8

DANGEROUS PREMISES

1.—THE PREMISES

The state of the premises

[Add to n.36]   **8–10**

In *Yates v National Trust* [2014] P.I.Q.R. P16, Ch.11, para.11-34, below, the
trial judge accepted that the defendant was not in breach of its duty as
occupier, where an employee of a tree surgeon fell from a tree on the
defendant's land, since the fall was caused by his pursuing the activity of tree
surgery and not as a result of the state of the defendant's premises.

The state of the premises

[Add to text after n.44]   **8–12**

... bannister rail.[44] In contrast, there was no "obvious danger" and therefore
no excuse for not warning of the risk of a fall where an informal path down
a slope at a castle ran close to a bastion wall and a sheer drop into a dry
moat.[44a]
NOTE 44a. *English Heritage v Taylor*[2016] EWCA Civ 448 (the Court was at
pains to point out that the decision turned upon its own facts, rejecting the
defendant's fear that public organisations permitting access to historic sites
would be under pressure to adopt an unduly defensive approach to the
protection of visitors, leading to an unwelcome proliferation of unsightly
warning signs).

2.—THE OCCUPIER

Multiple occupiers

[Add to text after n.80]   **8–20**

Although the defendant owned land on which hotel premises were situated,
and was a director of the company which operated the hotel, any duty as

[51]

CHAPTER 8

occupier was not so extensive as to make her liable for an accident caused by
a defective refrigerator located in an office of the hotel.[80a]
NOTE 80a. *Shtern v Cummings* [2014] UKPC 18 (she was not involved in the
day to day running of the business, which was the responsibility of the
company, although her ownership of the land may have given rise to a duty of
care in relation to the hotel's structure).

4. —THE DUTY OWED

(B) Extension, restriction, modification or exclusion of liability

Generally

8–43 [*Add to n.172*]

For changes to the Unfair Contract Terms Act 1977 on the coming into force
of the Consumer Rights Act 2015 see Ch.2, para.2-214, n.482a above. A
Legislative Note summarising the effect of the new provisions appears in
Appendix A to this Supplement.

(F) Defences

Business liability

8–74 [*Add footnote reference 278a to "s.2(3)" in the second line*]

NOTE 278a. The Unfair Contract Terms Act 1977 continues to apply to
contracts between businesses, notwithstanding the changes introduced by the
Consumer Rights Act 2015, which came into force on 1st October 2015: see
further Appendix A to this Supplement, and Ch.2, para.2-214, n.482a,
above.

(G) Effect of contract

Persons entering premises for the purpose of sport or entertainment

8–91 [*Add to text after n.316*]

A judge was entitled to conclude that where a company operating a sports ride
which involved the customer being propelled into the air by plastic ropes
while strapped into harness, there was a foreseeable risk of neck injury if he
was not properly warned before the mechanism was operated.[316a]
NOTE 316a. *Lowdon v Jumpzone Leisure UK Ltd* [2015] EWCA Civ 586
(there was a failure to follow the company's own guidelines which required
a count to three and a signal of readiness from the rider before the release).

8–92 [*Add to text after n.327*]

A stranger, apparently attempting to move a horsebox away from the parking
ground at the Hickstead Showground, raised the ramp on the claimant's
horsebox manually and when the claimant subsequently lowered it again

using the hydraulic system, he suffered serious injury: his claim against the occupiers of the Showground failed, inter alia, because there was a reasonable system in place to ensure vehicles had sufficient room in which to manoeuvre and the independent contractor employed to manage the parking area was not itself in breach of duty.[327a]
NOTE 327a. *Lear v Hickstead Ltd* [2016] EWHC 528 (QB), Picken J.

6.—LIABILITY OF VENDORS, LESSORS, BUILDERS AND LOCAL AUTHORITIES

(B) Statutory Liability

Landlord and Tenant Act 1985

[*Add to n.433*]   8–127

It is a necessary implication in the covenant implied by section 11 of the 1985 Act that the lessor, who is not in occupation of the property, can only be liable for disrepair within the demised premises of which he is aware: see *Edwards v Kumarasamy, The Times*, July 18, 2016, SC.

[*Add to n.442*]   8–129

In *Edwards v Kumarasamy, The Times*, July 18, 2016, SC, n.454, below, notwithstanding the landlord had a legal easement over the front hall of a block of flats, a paved area leading to the hall from the communal car park could not be described as part of the exterior of a building in which he had an estate or interest for purposes of s.11(1)(A).

[*Add to n.443*]

It was observed in *Edwards v Kumarasamy*, n.442, above, that the rule which required a landlord to have notice of a defect in the demised premises as a precondition to liability applied even where the defect arose in common parts of the building not themselves the subject of the letting, albeit technically the landlord retained a right of access over them.

[*Add to text after n.454*]   8–131

. . . a banister rail.[454]] A short paved area leading to the front door and hall of a block of flats from the adjacent car park was part of the structure or exterior of a flat within the block.[454a]
NOTE 454a. *Edwards v Kumarasamy* [2015] P.I.Q.R. P11, CA.

The Defective Premises Act 1972

[*Add to n.460*]   8–132

. . . windows, staircases, etc]: see *Rendlesham Estates plc v Barr Ltd.* [2015] B.L.R. 37, *per* Edwards-Stuart J. (individual apartments in apartment blocks were dwellings if they were places where a household lived to the exclusion of members of another household; also work to the common parts of the blocks was "in connection with the provision of a dwelling" since it was in connection with the provision of each apartment).

8–136 [*Add to n.472*]

There can be a breach of s.1 if when a building is completed there are defects which, if unrepaired, will subject the structural integrity of the building to a risk of failure during its design life. "Fit for habitation" means that, on completion, the building has to be capable of occupation for a reasonable time without risk to the occupants' health or safety and without undue discomfort or inconvenience to them: *Rendlesham Estates plc v Barr Ltd.*, n.460, above.

8–144 [*Add to the end of n.492*]

See also *Dodd v Raebarn Estates Ltd* [2016] EWHC 262 (QB); [2016] H.L.R. 12 where it was held that there was no breach of section 4 when the claimant was injured on steep stairs which did not have a handrail as the stairs, whilst possibly unsafe, were not "out of repair" and dangerousness was not the test under s.4 of the 1972 Act. To similar effect, also concerning a steep, dangerous, staircase see *Sternbaum v Dhesi* [2016] EWCA Civ 155; [2016] H.L.R. 16 at [29] *per* Hallett LJ "[g]iven the narrowness of the tread and the steepness of the flight of steps, particularly where it turns the corner, I have little doubt that, without a handrail, it was a hazard. But, as unsafe as it may have been, there is nothing about it that, to my mind, could possibly justify the description of being in disrepair. The walls and stairs themselves are apparently sound and there is nothing wrong with the floor covering."

7.—LIABILITY TO TRESPASSERS AND PERSONS OTHER THAN VISITORS

Discharges of duty and defences

8–169 [*Add to n.565*]

See Dickinson, "Open season for burglar battering: is it time to check in with the civil courts?" J.P.I. Law 2014, 2, 63 (compares the right of a homeowner to use reasonable force in self-defence as set out in the Criminal Justice and Immigration Act 2008 (c.4) s.76 and the Crime and Courts Act 2013 (c.22) s.43, with the duties of an occupier towards a trespasser under the Occupier's Liability Act 1984).

8.—LIABILITY TO PERSONS ON ADJOINING PREMISES

Liability to adjoining occupiers for progressive deterioration.

8–182 [*Add to n.595*]

. . . 13-167, below]; also *Coope v Ward* [2015] EWCA Civ 30, Ch.2, para.2-71, above (no breach of duty established where a wall between properties had collapsed without fault of either occupier, and it was not fair, just and reasonable to impose on one of them a liability to contribute to the unspecified cost of a replacement wall, where the wall was located on the other's land and the cause of the collapse lay on that other's side of the fence).

CHAPTER 9

PERSONS PROFESSING SOME SPECIAL SKILL

1.—ACTIONS AGAINST SKILLED PERSONS GENERALLY

The "Bolam" test

[Add to n.5]   9–02

The concept of professional status is an elastic one, see Mangan, "The curiosity of professional status" (2014) 2 PN 74; also (for an overview) Jackson, "The professions: power, privilege and legal liability" (2015) 3 PN 122 (the Peter Taylor Memorial Lecture).

Expert evidence

[Add new footnote reference 18a to "judge" in line 8]   9–05

NOTE 18a. See e.g. Graves v Brouwer [2015] EWCA Civ 595, Ch.5, para.5-47, above (in the context of an allegation that a fire in a house was caused by the defendant's negligence in setting an earlier fire in an alleyway, an expert was asked whether, if the court took the view that arson did not cause the house fire, then on the balance of probabilities, the alleyway fire had to be the cause, even if improbable: that was a question of mixed fact and law which was not the province of the witness).

[Add to line 3 of n.19]

. . . [1997] 1 All E.R. 577, CA at 601], also Kennedy v Cordia (Services) LLP [2016] UKSC 6, at [52]). [As to . . . .

[Add to text after n.21]

It is a precondition of the reception of expert evidence that there should be a reliable body of knowledge or experience to underpin it.[21a] Given the privileged position of an expert witness, a decision who is, or is not, to be treated as such has itself to be approached with care.

NOTE 21a. See *Kennedy v Cordia (Services) LLP* [2016] UKSC 6, Ch.12, at [44] (in the context of a claim for personal injury caused by a slip on an icy path, the Supreme Court considered the proper function and ambit of expert evidence).

Cause of action in both contract and tort

9–18 *[Add to the end of n.64]*

A tortious duty may also arise where professional services are rendered gratuitously, and no contract has come into being: *Burgess v Lejonvarn* [2016] EWHC 40 (an architect performing professional services for friends).

Remedies in Concurrent Duty Cases

9–22a *[Add new paragraph to text]*

In a concurrent duty case damages will be awarded on the contractual rather than tortious basis.[80a] Accordingly, the damage for which compensation will be given is that which was within the reasonable contemplation of the parties, a more restrictive test than the "reasonable foreseeability" test in tort.[80b] Whether the damage was within the reasonable contemplation of the parties will generally depend on the circumstances surrounding the creation of the contract. It has been suggested that the contractual remoteness standard should apply to cases in tort only where these case arise out of an assumption of responsibility, the classic "contract without consideration."[80c]

NOTE 80a. *Wellesley Partners v Withers* [2015] EWCA Civ 1146; [2016] P.N.L.R. 19 at [80], [163], [186].

NOTE 80b. See para.[74]. For a more detailed discussion of the contractual test see *Chitty on Contracts 32nd Edition*, Ch.26 s.7.

NOTE 80c. *Wellesley Partners v Withers*, above at para.[163].

2.—ACCOUNTANT AND AUDITORS

Scope of the contractual duty

9–24 *[Add to n.90]*

... 2013 4 PN 223]; also Wheeler, *"Mehjoo v Harben Barker*; specialist referrals in general accountancy practice-orthodoxy restored" (2014) 4 PN 195.

Duties to third parties in tort

9–38 *[Add to n.125]*

See *e.g. Swynson Ltd v Lowick Rose LLP* [2014] P.N.L.R. 27 (accountants who admitted negligence in preparing a due diligence report for a company considering whether to make a £10m loan did not owe a concurrent duty of care to the sole owner of the company even though it may have been foreseeable that his personal assets would be at stake).

[Add to text at the end of the paragraph]

... the accounts."[130]] The presence of a disclaimer can be an important part of the factual background when deciding whether, objectively speaking, auditors assumed responsibility to a third party for the accuracy of an audit report.[130a]
NOTE 130a. *Barclays Bank plc v Grant Thornton UK LLP* [2015] EWHC 320, Cooke J., Ch.2, para.2-215 above.

[Add to text after n.138]   **9–40**

A disclaimer appearing on the first page of a non-statutory audit report, which followed the standard wording produced by the Institute of Chartered Accountants in England & Wales in respect of statutory audits save for changing "the company's members" to "the company's director[s]", was held to prevent a duty of care arising to a third party bank in respect of the carrying out of a non-statutory audit.[138a] An accountant's does not owe a personal duty to a company director, notwithstanding that it is foreseeable that a director may suffer loss as a result of negligent accountancy advice.[138b]
NOTE 138a. *Barclays Bank plc v Grant Thornton UK LLP* [2015] EWHC 320 (Comm).
NOTE 138b. *Swynson Ltd v Lowick Rose LLP* [2014] P.N.L.R. 27, n.125 above; see also Ch.2, para.2-204a, above.

3.—ARCHITECTS, QUANTITY SURVEYORS, STRUCTURAL AND OTHER ENGINEERS, BUILDING CONTRACTORS

The duty of care

[Add to n.171]   **9–50**

... 14(6), 29. A duty of care may arise even though an architect acts gratuitously, no contract with the client having come into being: *Burgess v Lejonvarn* [2016] EWHC 40 (the architect chose a builder for friends and performed some project management in the expectation that a fee would be chargeable for a second phase of the proposed works once the initial phase was completed).

[Add to text after n.176]   **9–51**

Where architects provide a certificate of proper completion in relation to building works, which a purchaser does not rely upon in acquiring the property, there is no additional cause of action available for breach of a duty of care properly to inspect the works for purposes of preparing and issuing the certificate.[176a]
NOTE 176a. *Hunt v Optima (Cambridge) Ltd* [2014] P.N.L.R. 29, CA, Ch.2, para.2-195, above, *per* Tomlinson LJ at [114].

9–52   [*Add to text at the end of the paragraph*]

Without an assumption of responsibility a builder's duty in tort is to protect a client from personal injury or damage to other property. The duty can be owed not simply to the first person who acquires the property but also subsequent owners or users.[177a]

NOTE 177a. *Robinson v PE Jones (Contractors) Ltd*, n.177, above, *per* Jackson LJ at [68]. See further, Ch.2, para.2-251, and Ch.8, para.8-119, above. See also Carrington, "A crucial distinction" (2014) 4 PN 185.

The standard of care

9–72   [*Add to n.234*]

A construction company proposing to sink concrete piles on a site it was developing, was not negligent in failing to check museum archives before the concrete was laid to see whether there were any historic plans showing underground pipes not identified on current plans: *Northumbrian Water Ltd v Sir Robert McAlpine Ltd* [2014] EWCA Civ 685 (in fact the concrete escaped into a disused private drain, not shown on the claimant's plans, from which it made its way into the sewerage system maintained by the claimant).

4.—AUCTIONEERS

The duty of care

9–77   [*Add to text after n.253*]

... or the potentiality of such.[253] In the case of a leading auction house a higher standard of care and skill is required than a provincial house. It is to be expected that a work of art will be assessed by specialists with ready access to art historical scholarship around the world and given a thorough examination, over a sufficient period of time to come to a firm view as to its attribution where that is possible.[253a]

NOTE 253a. *Thwaytes v Sotheby's Ltd* [2015] P.N.L.R. 12 (defendant not negligent in failing to identify a painting, sold at auction for £42,000, as a Caravaggio worth many millions).

5.—BANKERS AND FINANCE COMPANIES

Giving advice or information

9–84   [*Add to text after n.272*]

... against him.[272] A bank was not liable to the claimant company, which operated a casino, when an employee negligently provided to the casino's agent a positive financial reference for a customer of the casino whose balance with the bank had always been nil. The bank was only aware that the reference was for the agent and unaware, either of the existence of the casino, or that the purpose of the reference was for gambling: no responsibility was assumed to

the casino; and it would not be fair, just and reasonable to impose a duty of care, given the casino's standard practice of concealing its existence and asking for references in the name of its agent.[272a]
NOTE 272a. *Playboy Club London Ltd v Banca Nazionale Del Lavoro SPA* [2016] EWCA Civ 457, Ch.2, para.2-195, above.

Proof of a causative link

[*Add to the end of n.294*]   **9–95**

... such instability]; also *Playboy Club London Ltd v Banca Nazionale Del Lavoro SPA* [2014] EWHC 2613 (QB), para.9–84, above.

6.—BARRISTERS

The standard of care

[*Add to text after n.319*]   **9–102**

... the decision.[319] It was negligent for a barrister to fail to advise parties with an interest in opposing a claim for judicial review to file evidence of prejudice at the preliminary stage when the applicants were seeking permission to commence the review proceedings. Nevertheless there was no damage where such evidence would have increased the prospects of resisting the application by only 5 to 10% and permission to proceed would probably have been given in any event.[319a] On the facts ....
NOTE 319a. *Thomas v Albutt* [2015] P.N.L.R. 29.

Wasted costs.

[*Note 329*]   **9–105**

Substitute para.9-254 for the reference to para.9-252 in the first line.

7.—DENTISTS

The duty of care

[*Add to n.341*]   **9–108**

... .the 1984 Act.] A claim for economic loss resulting from alleged negligence/breach of statutory duty in removing the claimant from the list of dentists approved to carry out NHS work, failed in *Jowhari v NHS England* [2014] EWHC 4197 (QB), Sir Colin Mackay.

8.—MEDICAL PRACTITIONERS

Diagnosis, treatment and advice about risks

[*Delete heading, text and footnotes from para.9–111 to 9–117 inclusive and replace as follows*]   **9–111**

In *Montgomery v Lanarkshire Health Board*[353] the Supreme Court identified the different approaches required when considering alleged negligence by a doctor, on the one hand in diagnosis or treatment and on the other in advising risks which the treatment may entail and the alternative strategies for treatment that are available. Diagnosis and treatment are areas of expertise susceptible to the traditional *Bolam* test[354], that is, did the medical practitioner act in a way that was accepted as proper by a responsible body of medical opinion. The test is otherwise in relation to advice about risks in treatment and alternatives. There the duty is to take reasonable care to ensure that, prior to treatment, the patient was aware of any material risks and any reasonable alternative to what was proposed.[355]

9–112   The claim in *Montgomery* arose as a result of severe injuries sustained by the claimant's son at the time of his birth. Mrs Montgomery was diabetic and small in stature. There was thereby a risk that her baby would have large shoulders and have difficulty passing through his mother's pelvis ("shoulder dystocia") without medical intervention. There was evidence that the risk if it materialised could give rise to a major obstetric emergency. In antenatal consultations Mrs Montgomery expressed concern about the size of her baby but did not seek advice about specific risks. The doctor did not volunteer such information because, in her judgment, the risk to the baby was very small and if it was mentioned the mother would elect caesarean section and that would not have be in her interests. She advised that mother would manage vaginal delivery and if there were difficulties in labour caesarean section would be given. In the event the risk of shoulder dystocia materialised in the course of the birth, the emergency which rapidly developed did not permit caesarean section, and the baby suffered injury in the course of delivery by forceps.

9–113   The appeal before the Supreme Court concerned allegations that Mrs Montgomery ought to have been given advice about the risk of shoulder dystocia which would arise in vaginal birth, and of the alternative possibility of delivery by elective caesarean section. The claimant had failed in the lower courts on an application of *Sidaway v Board of Governors of the Bethlem Royal Hospital and the Maudsley Hospital*,[356] a House of Lords' decision which was taken in effect to provide for a uniform approach, based on the *Bolam* principle, to cases of alleged medical negligence. The Supreme Court declined to follow that decision, indicating that the time had to review, in the light of changed social attitudes and medical practice, whether the *Bolam* test was suitable in considering a doctor's alleged failure to give proper advice about the risks of a particular course of treatment.

9–114   In the leading judgment Lords Kerr and Reed emphasised that it would be mistaken to regard *Sidaway* as rejecting any approach other than the *Bolam* test to "advice" cases. Nevertheless it appeared to give unjustified emphasis to whether a patient actually raised the issue of risks with the doctor. It achieved an unhappy compromise by applying *Bolam* as the primary test, but raising an exception that disclosure of a particular risk would be required if it was so obviously necessary to an informed choice on the part of the patient that no reasonably prudent medical man would fail to make it.[357] It was preferable to have an approach which reflected the fact that patients were adults "who are capable of understanding that medical treatment is uncertain of success and may involve risks, accepting responsibility for the taking of risks affecting their own lives, and living with the consequences of their choices."[358] There was a basic distinction between the doctor's role when providing, first, diagnosis or treatment and when, second, advising about risks and alternative treatments. So far as the first are concerned the doctor must follow the practice of ordinarily skilled members of his or her specialty. In relation to the second:

> "An adult person of sound mind is entitled to decide which, if any, of the available forms of treatment to undergo, and her consent must be obtained before treatment interfering with her bodily integrity is undertaken. The doctor is therefore under a duty to take reasonable care to ensure that the patient is aware of any material risks involved in any recommended treatment, and of any reasonable alternative or variant treatments. The test of materiality is whether, in the circumstances of the particular case, a reasonable person in the patient's position would be likely to attach significance to the risk, or the doctor is or should reasonably be aware that the particular patient would be likely to attach significance to it."

Two exceptions were allowed: **9–115**

> "The doctor is however entitled to withhold from the patient information as to a risk if he reasonably considers that its disclosure would be seriously detrimental to the patient's health. The doctor is also excused from conferring with the patient in circumstances of necessity, as for example where the patient requires treatment urgently but is unconscious or otherwise unable to make a decision. It is unnecessary for the purposes of this case to consider in detail the scope of those exceptions."

On the facts Mrs Montgomery should have been informed of the risks of shoulder dystocia and the evidence suggested that, had this occurred, she would have elected delivery of her baby by caesarean section and the injuries in question would not have arisen.[359]

NOTE 353. [2015] 2 W.L.R. 768, SC. This important decision means that many cases referred to in the existing text come with a "health warning" in terms of precedent. See further, McGrath, "Trust me, I'm a patient . . . : disclosure standards and the patient's right to decide" C.L.J. 2015, 74(2), 211; Bagshaw, "Modernising the doctor's duty to disclose risks of treatment" L.Q.R. 2016, 132(Apr), 182.

NOTE 354. *Bolam v Friern Hospital Management Committee* [1957] 1 WLR 582, 587. See para.9–125, below.

NOTE 355. See below para.9–114.

NOTE 356. [1985] A.C. 871.

NOTE 357. This aspect of *Sidaway* received some further development in *Pearce v United Bristol Healthcare NHS Trust* [1998] P.I.Q.R. P53, CA, particularly *per* Lord Woolf at P59.

NOTE 358. In *Chester v Afshar* [2005] 1 A.C. 134 Lord Walker of Gestingthorpe referred to a warning of risks being an aspect of the advice which a doctor was under a duty to give (at [92]). He also observed that during the years which had elapsed since *Sidaway,* the importance of personal autonomy had been increasingly recognised.

NOTE 359. The claimant had lost on the causation issue in the lower courts but the Supreme Court reviewed it in her favour in light of the finding that had the doctor properly discharged her duty advice would have been given that caesarean section was available as an alternative method of delivery.

CHAPTER 9

Necessity of the patient's consent

9–117a *[Add new paragraph to text]*

Border v Lewisham and Greenwich NHS Trust[368a] was a claim where no consent had been obtained to the insertion of a cannula into the left arm of a patient, who subsequently developed infection at the site and suffered permanent disability as a result. The trial judge found that in the particular circumstances the doctor had, in inserting the cannula, acted in accordance with the practice of a recognised body of medical opinion and was not negligent. On appeal it was held that a finding of breach of duty was inevitable once it was found consent had not been given, since it was implicit in the duty to warn of the risks of a treatment that consent should be obtained. The case was remitted to the judge for a finding whether, had consent been sought, the patient would have agreed.[368b]

NOTE 368a. [2015] Med. L.R. 48, CA.

NOTE 368b. It should perhaps be noted that the case had its difficulties in terms of how the issue of consent arose. At first instance the claimant did not advance the argument which subsequently found favour in the Court of Appeal. The expert evidence at trial appears to have addressed the correctness of inserting the cannula at once rather than waiting to see if it was required. It was not argued before the trial judge that if consent was not obtained, that was itself negligent, leaving only the issue of causation.

Duty to third parties

9–123a *[Add new paragraph to text]*

A medical practitioner does not owe a duty to non-patients where it is alleged that a failure to promptly diagnose a patient's illness led to delayed diagnosis of a third party's own illness. In *ABC v St George's Healthcare NHS Foundation Trust*[379a] it was held that no duty was owed to inform a pregnant relative of the diagnosis of a genetic disease that could affect an unborn child, even in circumstance where the claimant made clear that she would have terminated the pregnancy had she known at the relevant time. In particular, the court would not impose a duty which would interfere with the duty of confidentiality owed by a doctor to his or her patients. In *Smith v University of Leicester*[379b] it was held that no duty was owed to claimants who were not patients of the defendant and whose diagnosis with a genetic disorder had been delayed due to the defendant's delayed diagnosis of the same disorder in a second cousin.[379c]

NOTE 379a. [2015] P.I.Q.R. P18.

NOTE 379b. [2016] EWHC 817 (QB).

NOTE 379c. *Per* HHJ McKenna, sitting as a judge of the High Court, at [29]: "a third party cannot recover damages for a personal injury suffered because of an omission in the treatment of another."

9–124 *[Add to n.382]*

See further *CN v Poole Borough Council* [2016] EWHC 569 (QB).

Clinical judgment

[*Add to text at the end of the paragraph*]   **9–129**

It should be recognised in assessing the standard of care provided in hospitals that clinical judgments may have to be formulated in rushed or hurried circumstances where the opportunities for reflection, research, or consultation with other colleagues may be limited.[403a]
NOTE 403a. See e.g. *Mulholland v Medway NHS Foundation Trust* [2015] EWHC 268 (hospital GP in the A&E department not negligent in failing to diagnose the claimant as a risk of a stroke).

Setting the standard of care

[*Add to text after n.412*]   **9–131**

. . . patient not informed;[412]] where a surgeon failed to detect a blob of cement left in contact with the sciatic nerve in the course of a total hip replacement operation[412a]; [where a doctor . . . .
NOTE 412a. *Royal Wolverhampton Hospitals NHS Trust v Evans* [2015] EWCA Civ 1059 (it was common ground that it was not evidence of sub-standard surgical technique that an extrusion of cement occurred; but the fact that it could occur called for a high degree of vigilance to ensure that excess cement was not left behind).

[*Add to text after n.419*]

. . . delayed[419]]; where a doctor failed to administer and elicit results from the three necessary tests for diagnosing a scaphoid fracture.[419a]
NOTE 419a. *Arkless v Betsi Cadwaladr University Local Health Board* [2016] EWHC 330 (QB).

Mentally disordered patients

[*Add to n.468*]   **9–141**

. . . sustained injury]; also *Webley v St George's Hospital NHS Trust* (2014) 108 B.M.L.R. 190 (failing actively to guard a patient who had been sectioned and was known to present a high risk of absconding).

9.—HOSPITALS AND HEALTH AUTHORITIES

The duty of care.

[*Add to text after n.516*]   **9–157**

. . . .German hospital[516]] No duty of care was owed by hospitals treating the claimant's father, to inform her that he had been diagnosed with Huntingdon's disease, a genetic condition, and that there was a 50% chance she would develop the disease herself.[516a]
NOTE 516a. *ABC v St George's Healthcare NHS Foundation Trust* [2015] P.I.Q.R. P18, Ch.2, para.2-68a, above. See also *Smith v University of Leicester NHS Trust* [2016] EWHC 817 (QB), HHJ McKenna (no duty of care

established to diagnose earlier a patient's adrenomyeloneuropathy, a complex genetic disease which adversely impacts upon the myelin or white matter of the brain, thereby leading to an earlier diagnosis of the condition in two boys, his second cousins).

9–158a   [*Add new paragraph to text*]

There is no duty of care to prevent patients leaving a hospital accident and emergency department before they are triaged by providing an accurate estimate of the time within which the patient will be seen. It would not be fair, just and reasonable to impose such a duty, which would be likely to result in refusal by reception staff to estimate a waiting time; would impinge on clinical judgments by which patients may be seen in order of seriousness; and might lead to reduced efficacy in the functions of accident and emergency receptionists. Further it would not be fair just and reasonable to impose liability where the decision to leave was ultimately that of the patient, not the hospital.[517a]
NOTE 517a. *Darnley v Croydon Health Services NHS Trust* [2016] P.I.Q.R. P4. In coming to its conclusion the court relied in part upon the restatement of the rules surrounding assessments of fairness, justice and reasonableness found at Ch.2, paras. 2-40, 2-41 above.

10.—INSURANCE AGENTS AND BROKERS

The standard of care

9–181   [*Add to text after n.602*]

... substantial dispute.[602] Brokers were liable where they failed to advise companies, who sold payment protection insurance, to make a block notification of PPI sales at the earliest opportunity, leading to excess cover being refused.[602a]
NOTE 602a. *Ocean Finance & Mortgages Ltd v Senior Wright Ltd* [2016] EWHC 160 (Comm).

9–182a   [*Add new paragraph to text*]

The standard of care required of an insurance broker instructed to arrange business interruption insurance cover was considered in *Eurokey Recycling Ltd v Giles Insurance Brokers Ltd.*[612a] It was observed, summarising the effect of a number of authorities, that the nature and scope of a broker's obligation to assess a client's business interruption insurance needs depended on the particular circumstances, including the client's sophistication. The level of client sophistication would vary enormously and it could not be assumed that small and medium enterprises, for example, would understand the nature of the insurance. Although annual repetition of advice previously given would not be required, that assumed that the responsible personnel remained the same and that the giving of the advice could be properly demonstrated by documentation or otherwise. If a client who appeared to be well-informed about his business provided a broker with information, the broker was not expected to verify that information unless he had reason to believe that it was not accurate. While a broker was not expected himself to calculate the business interruption sum insured or to choose an indemnity period, he had to provide sufficient explanation to enable the client to do so. Such explanation should include the method of calculating the sum insured, and might well require an explanation of terms such as "estimated gross profits", "maximum indemnity period", and the relevant considerations when choosing a maximum indemnity period. The broker would need to take reasonable steps to ascertain the nature of the client's business and its insurance needs, but if providing the same type of service as in the instant case, was neither required nor expected to conduct a detailed investigation into a client's business. NOTE 612a. [2015] P.N.L.R. 5, Blair J.

13.—SCHOOLS AND SCHOOLTEACHERS

The duty of care

[Add to n.629]   **9–187**

... service).] See Giliker, "Vicarious liability, non-delegable duties and teachers: can you outsource liability for lessons?" (2015) 4 PN 259.

Supervision of games or playing

[Add to text at the end of the paragraph]   **9–197**

It was negligent for a teacher supervising children at a swimming pool to be unaware for at least thirty seconds that the claimant, a ten-year-old child, was in difficulties in the water.[663a]
NOTE 663a. *Woodland v Maxwell* [2015] EWHC 273 (QB), Ch.3, para.3-196, above.

Knowledge of dangerous games

[Add to text at the end of the paragraph]   **9–203**

... injury.[688]] A school was not liable to a pupil, not wearing a mouth guard, who suffered dental injuries during a game of hockey, the use of mouth guards being encouraged but not mandatory.[688a]
NOTE 688a. *Murray v McCullough* [2016] NIQB 52, Stephens J (the school followed the practice of both the governing body of the sport and other schools, and the pupil was sufficiently mature to appreciate the risks of not wearing a mouth guard, and to weigh those risks against the inconvenience of using it).

14.—SOLICITORS

(B) The standard of care

Importance of the retainer

[Add to n.807]   **9–235**

... the will's validity]. *Per* Patten LJ in *Mehjoo v Harben Barker* [2014] P.N.L.R. 24, CA at [34]: "there is no such thing as a general retainer and the

terms and limits of the retainer and any consequent duty of care therefore
depend upon what the professional is instructed to do."

[*Add new footnote reference 809a to "understood" in line 10*]

Note 809a. It was negligent to take instructions from a client with a damages
for personal injury claim by sending him several long, standardised letters to
which he was to respond by ticking boxes: instructions should have been
taken in a way that allowed gave clarity whether he had understood the
potential extent of his claim: *Proctor v Raleys Solicitors* [2015] EWCA Civ
400 (the client was unsophisticated in the relevant field; the written advice
given to him was unclear; and there were clear indications that he might not
have understood that advice).

9–236 [*Add to text at the end of the paragraph*]

... circumstances required.[815] In circumstances where a firm acting in a
group action has responsibility for receiving a settlement sum, for safeguarding it pending distribution and for distributing it to the proper recipients,
their retainer will extend to managing the risks involved in doing so, which
should include an assessment of the political and other risks to which the
settlement sum was vulnerable.[815a]
Note 815a. *Agouman v Leigh Day* [2016] EWHC 1324 (QB), Andrew Smith
J, at [82].

9–236a [*Add new paragraph to text*]

Where a solicitor was asked to draft a consent order for the court's approval
in matrimonial proceedings, the parties having at that stage come to terms, it
was not negligent to fail to advise her client about alleged shortcomings in the
settlement. The retainer was a limited one and the provision of additional
advice or warning was not reasonably incidental to the work instructed. It was
relevant that the client was an intelligent woman who had practised as a
chartered accountant. She had, as the solicitor knew, already taken legal
advice about the proposed consent order before instructions were given, and
had rejected the solicitor's warning about the difficulties of enforcement if her
husband emigrated. She had made it plain that, despite the risks, she wished
to conclude the consent order as swiftly as possible.[815b]
Note 815b. *Minkin v Landsberg* [2016] 1 W.L.R. 1489, CA. *Per* King LJ, it
was important that where a solicitor acted on a limited retainer, client care
letters, attendance notes and formal written retainers were drafted with
considerable care to reflect the client's specific instructions.

See also *BPC Hotels Ltd v Wright Hassall LLP* [2016] EWHC 1286 (TCC)
(*Miniken* applied where it was alleged that solicitors had failed to identify a
particular ground of claim against the claimant's former solicitors).

Illustrations of liability

9–249 [*Add to text after n.888*]

... to be made absolute;[888] failing timeously to agree an order for ancillary
relief and obtain decree absolute for a client in matrimonial proceedings so

that the order eventually obtained was rendered of no effect by the respondent's bankruptcy;[888a] [failing to prosecute effectively . . .
NOTE 888a. *Stewart v Patterson Donnelly Solicitors* [2015] P.N.L.R. 7.

[*Add to text after n.891*]

..named;[891] failing to clarify with a client why he had chosen not to pursue a claim for a head of loss which had been identified as likely to be recoverable, where it was foreseeable that the client might not understand the information communicated by the solicitor about his entitlement to claim[891a] failing to protect monies received in settlement of a client's personal injury claim.[891b]
NOTE 891a. *Proctor v Raleys Solicitors* [2015] EWCA Civ 400.
NOTE 891b. *Agouman v Leigh Day* [2016] EWHC 1324 (QB), Andrew Smith J (a reasonable solicitor could not properly have decided to leave the settlement sum in an Ivorian account pending distribution, and should have arranged to move it once it was clear that ruthless and violent individuals were interested in it: [82]-[113]).

Illustrations of no liability

[*Add to text after n.895*]   **9–250**

It was not negligent prior to *XYZ v Various Companies* [2013] EWHC 3643 for solicitors acting for a party with a substantial counterclaim, to fail to seek an order from the court that information be provided by the defendant to the counterclaim about its ability to meet an order for damages and costs.[895a]
NOTE 895a. *Dowling v Bennett Griffin* [2014] EWCA Civ 1545 (it was observed by Sullivan LJ that if in earlier cases two High Court judges had taken the view, after argument, that there was no power to order the disclosure of insurance information it could scarcely be negligent of the solicitors to take the same view).

Wasted costs.

[*Add to n.929*]   **9–257**

. . . at 578.] In *Kagalovsky v Balmore Invest Ltd* [2015] P.N.L.R. 26 an application for wasted costs was dismissed where it was "demonstratively unsuitable" for summary application, given in particular that it involved an allegation of participation in a client's fraud, and that the matters complained of did not arise in the face of the court.

[*Add to text after n.985*]   **9–267**

. . . deposit[985]]; when acting in the purchase of land including a right of way over a lane which gave access, failing to make further investigations when pre contract enquiries indicated that the seller had no knowledge of any adverse claims, albeit in fact a third party had made claims in relation to the use and ownership of the lane;[985a] [in failing to advise . . .
NOTE 985a. *Young v Hamilton* [2014] P.N.L.R. 30, CA (NI).

Duty when money is being lent

[*Add to text after n.1015*]   **9–271**

. . . the transaction[1015]]; should have realised that the date of purchase and price paid for the property strongly suggested that the surveyors' valuation

was greatly excessive and reported this to the lender, as a necessary incident of the solicitors duty to investigate and report on title.[1015a]
NOTE 1015a. *E.Surv Ltd v Goldsmith Williams Solicitors* [2016] 4 W.L.R. 44, CA.

(C) Causation and Damage

"Wrong information" claims

9–283   *[Add to text after n.1054]*

Also, where a solicitor who had drawn up a loan agreement for a client, failed to inform him that the money he was advancing was being used for a purpose other than that he intended, there was a breach of duty, but no liability for the client's losses when the loan was not repaid because they did not fall within the scope of the duty.[1054a]
NOTE 1054a. *Gabriel v Little* [2013] EWCA Civ 1513.

Application of SAAMCO

9–285   *[Add new paragraph to text]*

SAAMCO was applied in *LSREF III Wight Ltd v Gateley LLP*[1060a], a claim arising from solicitors delete failing to report accurately on title when acting for a bank which was advancing a loan on security of the lease of a property subject to a first legal charge. When enforcing its security the bank discovered that the lease was, as a result of the charge, worth considerably less than anticipated. The principal issue on appeal was the date at which the loss should be assessed. It was held that the first step was to identify whether loss had been suffered from entering into the transaction (transactional loss); and the second, what part of that loss was properly attributable to the solicitors' negligence. The first step did not have to be carried out as at the date of the transaction: the court would not blind itself from knowledge of relevant facts occurring thereafter. A lender's transactional loss would be most easily identified once it had crystallised by realisation of the security and the application of the proceeds to the outstanding debt. Where the transactional loss of someone who had loaned money on negligent advice remained uncrystallised at the date of trial, it would be a rare case in which a quantification of that loss would be better calculated by reference to any earlier date than the trial date. Even though a lender could be shown to have suffered some immediate loss on the transaction date, that did not conclude the question whether that would prove to be its real transactional loss.
NOTE 1060a. [2016] EWCA Civ 359. (A separate issue whether the loss could and should have been mitigated by negotiating a variation of the lease was resolved in favour of the defendants).

Claims arising from the acquisition of property

9–287   *[Add to the end of n.1070]*

See *e.g. Bacciottini v Gotelee & Goldsmith* [2016] EWCA Civ 170, Ch.5, para.5-54, above (nominal damages only where solicitors failed to identify a planning restriction on a conveyance of land, but the value of the land was in the event unaffected).

Other claims arising from the negligent conduct of non-contentious business

[Add to n.1081]   **9–293**

See also *Gabriel v Little* [2013] EWCA Civ 1513, n.1054, above (a loan case where the solicitor was in breach of the duty to provide information, but was not responsible for losses incurred when the loan was not repaid).

16.—Valuers, Estate Agents and Surveyors

[*Note 1136*]   **9–311**

Harrison v Technical Sign Co Ltd reported at [2014] P.N.L.R. 15.

[*Add to text after n.1136*]

A duty of care did not arise as between a tree surgeon contracted to a landowner to clear dead wood from a 150-year-old ash tree and a railway company one of whose trains was damaged when, three years later, one of the remaining limbs of the tree fell onto the adjacent railway line: any duty in tort to the claimant could not extend further than the contractual obligation to the landowner, which did not require the defendant to give advice about the general state of the tree unless, for instance, he discovered something clearly dangerous.[1136a]
Note 1136a. *Stagecoach South Western Trains v Hind* [2014] E.G.L.R. 59, Ch.10, para.10-22, below.

[*Add to text after n.1147*]   **9–315**

The surveyor's valuation.[1147] A valuer employed by a company did not assume personal responsibility for a valuation of property by including in his valuation report the words "the valuer accepts responsibility" to the client: it was clear from its overall tenor that the report was submitted by the company and the company's logo was stamped below the defendant's signature.[1147a]
Note 1147a. *Bush v Summit Advances Ltd* [2015] P.N.L.R. 18.

Valuers and estate agents

[*Delete text in n.1172 from"applying" in line 7 to "above" in line 8*]   **9–322**

[*Add to the end of n.1172*]

. . . adding a rider to it.] See also *Helm Housing Ltd v Myles Danker Associates Ltd* [2016] P.N.L.R. 4 (*per* Horner J: "In this case the valuation under consideration was a one-off valuation for a single site without any obvious exceptional features. There was a reliable comparable transaction provided by the sale of the index site a few months before. There were other comparable transactions available although these were off market and of much more limited weight. This was not and should not have been a complex matter. Accordingly I consider that the issue . . . is whether the valuation of this site falls within the broad range of plus or minus 10 per cent..").

CHAPTER 10

HIGHWAYS AND TRANSPORT

1.—HIGHWAYS

(A) Maintenance of the highway

The Highways Act 1980

10–03   [*Add to the end of n.14*]

The duty under s.41 does not include a duty to ensure the highway is clear of moss, algae, lichen or similar vegetation: *Rollinson v Dudley* [2016] P.I.Q.R. P6.

(B) Dangers in the highway

Trees and shrubs

10–22   [*Add to n.77*]

See further *Stagecoach South Western Trains Ltd v Hind* [2014] E.G.L.R. 59, *per* Coulson J., "I can see no basis in the authorities for the proposition that a reasonable and prudent landowner is obliged, as a matter of course and without any trigger or warning sign, to pay for an arboriculturalist to carry out periodic inspections of the trees on his or her land. In my view, that is coming far too close to making the landowner an insurer of nature." He went on to say that the authorities proceeded on the basis that a closer inspection of a tree by an expert was only required where something was revealed by an informal or preliminary inspection which gave rise to a cause for concern.

[*Add to text after n.79*]

... not liable.[79] An educated and enthusiastic gardener with some knowledge of trees, who carried out regular informal inspections of the trees in her garden, was not in breach of duty in failing to heed or act upon the potential danger from an "included bark" union of stems of an ash tree where the tree was apparently healthy, access was difficult and the trunk covered in ivy.[79a] [Conversely ...

NOTE 79a. *Stagecoach South Western Trains v Hind* n.77 above. One of the stems of the tree fell onto a railway line and damaged a train, having

[70]

developed a crack at the included bark union. It was emphasised that the duty of the landowner was to act reasonably and prudently and that duty had been discharged by her informal inspections.

Statutory obligation to light

[Add footnote reference 162a to "itself" in line 3]   **10–53**

NOTE 162a. The view has been expressed that Scots law may be more generous to claimants when considering the liability of a local authority to provide street lighting: *Macdonald v Comhairle Nan Eilean Siar* [2015] CSOH 132, Lord Matthews.

2.—CARRIERS

(C) Road Carriage

Stopping and starting

[Add to n.441]   **10–147**

. . . not to alight prematurely]; *Steel v McGill's Bus Service Ltd* 2015 Rep. L.R. 39, OH (liability for injury suffered by an 82-year-old lady where a bus moved off before reached her seat).

Child safety seats

[Add to n.477]   **10–159**

. . . (SI 2006/2213)] See further the Motor Vehicles (Wearing of Seat Belts by Children in Front Seats) (Amendment) Regulations 2015/402, in force 28 March 2015.

(D) Ships

The Athens Convention

[Add new footnote 288a to "years" in line 3]   **10–164**

NOTE 288a. In relation to the construction of arts.14 and 16 of the Athens Convention of 1974 see *per* Lord Macmillan in *Stag Line v Foscolo Mango & Co Ltd* [1932] A.C. 328, quoted at Ch. 4, n.296, above.

(E) Aircraft

Accident

[Note 545]   **10–184**

Ford v Malaysian Airline Systems Berhad reported at [2014] 1 Lloyd's Rep. 301, CA.

[Add to n.545 after the case reference]

It was said that if a cause that led to the claimant's physical reaction was an event that was external to her and was one that was unusual from her perspective, that would bring the circumstances within the description of an accident: on the facts however the event, that is the administration of an injection by a doctor, was not unusual and no accident arose).

Delay

10–188a   *[Add new paragraph to text]*

Claims for compensation for cancelled or delayed flights have become a fruitful source of litigation and it is not proposed here to deal with the subject in a comprehensive way, for which the reader must turn to specialist works.[556a] Nevertheless such claims have exposed a problem in reconciling the approach taken to the Warsaw (subsequently the Montreal) Convention by the House of Lords in *Sidhu v British Airways*[556b] and the approach of the European Court of Justice to claims for delay brought under EC Regulation, and a brief summary of the difficulty is required.

10–188b   Under the Montreal Convention 1999 a right to compensation for delay is given, subject to provisions limiting the amount of recovery and a two year limitation period for claims.[556c] In 2004 the European Union, notwithstanding that it is a party to the Montreal Convention, published EC Regulation No. 261/2004 which itself includes remedies for cancellation, prevention of boarding and delay.[556d] The remedy for delay has been interpreted by the European Court as including a right to compensation where the delay in arrival exceeded three hours.[556e] Challenges to the Regulation on the basis that it is inconsistent with the Convention, have failed.[556f] It was also decided that the limitation period applying to claims for delay under the Regulation were a matter for national law.[556g] The two year period under the Convention did not apply. The Court of Appeal has ruled that to the extent that the approach taken in the European Court differs from the reasoning in *Sidhu*, the European decisions must, in this jurisdiction, be preferred and applied.[556h]

NOTE 556a. See articles, N.L.J. 2014, 164 (7629), 5; S. & T.I. 2014, 10(2), 36; S.J. 2014, 158(26), 9.

NOTE 556b. [1997] A.C. 430, n.555, above.

NOTE 556c. See art.19— Delay. "The carrier is liable for damage occasioned by delay in the carriage by air of passengers, baggage or cargo . . . "

NOTE 556d. See art.4: "(i) . . . if a passenger is denied boarding against his will, the airline must pay compensation in a prescribed amount in accordance with article 7 and offer assistance in the form of reimbursement or re-routing in accordance with article 8, as well as meals and refreshment, transport and hotel accommodation and two free telephone calls in accordance with article 9; art.5: (ii) . . . if a flight is cancelled, the airline must offer passengers prescribed compensation, reimbursement or re-routing and assistance in accordance with articles 7, 8 and 9; article 6: (iii) . . . if an airline reasonably expects a flight to be delayed beyond its schedules time of departure by two hours or more (depending on the distance of the flight involved), it must offer passengers assistance in accordance with art.9 and in extreme cases reimbursement in accordance with art.8."

NOTE 556e *Sturgeon v Condor Flugdienst G.m.b.H.* (Cases C-402/07 and C-432/07), [2012] 2 All E.R. (Comm) 983.
NOTE 556f *International Air Transport Association (IATA) v Department for Transport* (Case C-344/04) [2006] 2 C.M.L.R. 20.
NOTE 556g *Cuadrench Moré v Koninklijke Luchtvaart Maatschappij N.V.* (Case C-139/11), [2013] 2 All E.R. (Comm) 1152.
NOTE 556h. *Dawson v Thomson Airways Ltd* [2015] 1 W.L.R. 883, CA.

3.—HIGHWAY USERS AND COLLISIONS

Police

[*Add to n.655*] **10–214**

. . . causative significance]; appeal dismissed [2013] EWCA Civ 1477. See Fisher, "*Boyle v Commissioner of Police of the Metropolis*" J.P.I. Law 2014, 1, C5.

Contributory negligence of passengers

[*Add to n.814*] **10–268**

See also *McCracken v Smith* [2015] EWCA Civ 380, Ch.4, para.4-261, above.

Pedal cyclists

[*Add to text after "balance" in the second last line*] **10–270**

which may adversely affect balance.] A cyclist who rode her bicycle in the centre of the road on a bend where an oncoming car had only a limited ability to appreciate the hazard she presented, was guilty of contributory negligence, assessed at 25%.[824a]
NOTE 824a. *Sinclair v Joyner* [2015] R.T.R. 29, Cox J.

Pedestrians

[*Add to n.829*] **10–272**

; also *Sabir v Osei-Kwabena* [2016] P.I.Q.R. Q4, CA (a pedestrian who should have seen a car and clearly misjudged its position contributed to her accident by 25%; the car driver who was travelling at 30mph but did not see her until she was three or four metres away was principally to blame).

[*Add to n.844*] **10–276**

See also *Jackson v Murray* [2015] 2 All E.R. 805, SC, Ch.4, para.4-40, above (50% contributory negligence where a 13-year-old child moved into the path of a car from behind a school bus).

EMPLOYMENT AT COMMON LAW

1.—COMMON LAW DUTY OF EMPLOYER

(A) Introduction

Generally

11–01 *[Add to line 3 of n.1 after the case reference]*

... P17, CA,] also *Thompson v Renwick Group Plc* [2014] P.I.Q.R. P18 [Ch.2, para.2-82, above.

[Add new footnote reference 1a to "employment" in the last line]

NOTE 1a. For the meaning of the phrase "course of employment", see Ch.3, para.3-119 ff, above. See also e.g. *Vaughan v Ministry of Defence* [2015] EWHC 1404 (QB), William Davis J. (a marine on a training exercise, who on a day off, suffered injury when he dived into shallow water was not on duty, not acting in the course of his employment and the defendant owed him no duty of care *qua* employer).

Nature of the duty

11–02 *[Add to text after n.13]*

It has been observed that in modern times it is no longer appropriate to speak of an employer's duty being confined to "such precautions as are ordinarily taken", or "such other precautions as are so obviously wanted that it would be folly in anyone to neglect to provide them."[13a] "A negligent omission can result from a failure to seek out knowledge of risks which are not in themselves obvious."[13b]

NOTE 13a. *Per* Lord Dunedin in *Morton v William Dixon Ltd* 1909 S.C. 807, quoted below at para.11-71.

NOTE 13b. *Per* Lords Reed and Hodge SCJs in *Kennedy v Cordia (Services) LLP* [2016] UKSC 6 at [111]. See further Ch.12, para.12-256, below.

Economic Harm.

11–04 *[Add to text after n.25]*

... insurance scheme.[25]] An employer does not owe a duty to employees to prevent the development of a condition (platinum sensitisation) not amounting to physical injury where this may lead to reduced earning capacity in future.[25a]

NOTE 25a. *Greenway v Johnson Matthey plc* [2016] EWCA Civ 408, in particular at [46]-[51].

Statutory duty to insure

[*Add to n.36*]   **11–07**

Richardson v Pitt-Stanley has been applied in Scotland, see *Campbell v Peter Gordon Joiners Ltd* 2015 S.L.T. 134 (the claimant, who was injured when using an unguarded circular saw in the course of his employment by a company which had no funds to meet his claim, failed in his claim against the sole director, who he alleged was in breach of a qualified duty of care not to permit the company to carry on business without there being in place an insurance policy as required by the Employers' Liability (Compulsory Insurance) Act 1969). Appeal dismissed [2016] UKSC 38.

Relevance of the contractual relationship

[*Add to text after n.45*]   **11–09**

... employee in contract.[45] In contrast, in *Greenway v Johnson Matthey plc* it was held that the absence of express or implied contractual terms protecting employees from financial loss due to platinum sensitisation was an important consideration in denying a duty of care in negligence to prevent such economic loss.

> "Where the nexus between parties is founded in a contractual relationship, as here, it is the contract which they have made with each other which is the primary source and reference point for the rights they have and the obligations they owe each other. Although a duty of care in tort may run in parallel with the contractual duty and have the same content, it is difficult to see how the law of tort could impose obligations in this area which are more extensive than those given by interpretation of the contract which the parties have made for themselves. The usual rule is that freedom of contract is paramount, and if the parties have agreed terms to govern their relationship which do not involve the assumption of responsibility by the employer for some particular risk, the general law of tort will not operate to impose on the employer an obligation which is more extensive than that which they agreed ... Since there is no implied contractual term according to which Johnson Matthey is obliged to protect the appellants in relation to their financial losses arising in the circumstances of this case, so equally there can be no duty in tort to protect them in relation to the pure economic loss they have suffered by reason of those financial losses."[45a]

NOTE 45a. *Greenway v Johnson Matthey plc* [2016] EWCA Civ 408, *per* Sales LJ at [49]-[51]

(B) Elements of the duty

(i) *Safe place of work*

[*Add new paragraph to text*]   **11–23a**

The employer's personal duty to take reasonable care to ensure that an employee is reasonably safe from injury extends to travel abroad, even where the means of travel is under the control of third parties. So, where one of the

CHAPTER 11

defendant's senior managers was among those killed on a helicopter flight in Peru, and the company failed to make adequate or sufficient enquiry about the safety of the journey, the employer was liable, even though it was the defendant's client, which was developing the site, which was also responsible for selecting the firm from which to charter the helicopter.[113a] Also, where the deceased, a financier, took a charter flight from Cameroon to the Republic of Congo, and the 'plane crashed, his employers were in breach of duty in failing to make appropriate enquiries about safety, even though the flight was arranged by a third party, although causation was not established where those enquiries would not have revealed matters of concern.[113b]

NOTE 113a. *Dusek v Stormharbour Securities LLP* [2015] EWHC 37 (QB) (*per* Hamblen J at [174]: "The proposed flight raised obvious and foreseeable safety risks. The essential nature of the risk was unsafe operation or performance of the helicopter flight. Further, there was a real prospect of that risk eventuating given the challenging nature of the flight. Yet further, if such risk did eventuate the likely consequence was catastrophic, namely death or at least serious personal injury." Had a safety audit been carried out the conclusion would have been that the deceased was advised not to go on the flight and he would not have done so).

NOTE 113b. *Cassley v GMP Securities Europe LLP* [2015] EWHC 722 (QB), Coulson J.

Employee gaining access to or working on another's premises or plant

11–34   [*Note 144*]

Yates v National Trust reported at [2014] P.I.Q.R. P16.

Nature of the duty

11–74a   [*Add new paragraph to text*]

While a chief constable owes police officers within his force a non-delegable duty to provide a safe system of work, which would extend in appropriate circumstances to a duty to warn them of some danger, that duty can be displaced as a matter of public policy,[292a] or because it would be not fair, just and reasonable for such a duty to exist. Such was the case where an officer was shot and seriously injured by a fugitive offender some seven minutes after a 999 call had been received, in which the offender issued threats against the police in general and said he was coming to get them.[292b]

NOTE 292a. *Hill v Chief Constable of West Yorkshire* [1989] A.C. 53, Ch.2, para.2-311, above.

NOTE 292b. *Rathband v Chief Constable of Northumbria* [2016] EWHC 181 (QB), Males J. (although a duty of care was rejected in principle, it was made clear that on the facts the decision of a senior officer to obtain an urgent cell-site analysis and to listen to the call again before any warning was issued, was reasonable).

Safe system of work

11–85   [*Add to text after n.357*]

... other workmen;[357]] where a military contractor had not imposed strict fitness requirements on interpreters before they could take part in a training exercise.[357a]

NOTE 357a. *Humphrey v Aegis Defence Services Ltd* [2016] EWCA Civ 11, Ch.7, above at para.7-33.

Stress at work

[Add to the end of n.362]   **11–87**

See also *Yapp v Foreign and Commonwealth Office* [2015] I.R.L.R. 112, CA (a claim based upon psychiatric injury suffered by a diplomat who was withdrawn from his role after an allegation, later found to be unsubstantiated, that he had behaved in a manner likely to damage the reputation of the United Kingdom. In the course of an extensive review of earlier cases it was pointed out that it would be generally regarded as exceptional for an apparently robust employee, with no history of psychiatric ill health, to develop a depressive illness as a result of even a very serious setback at work. There was nothing about the instant case that was sufficiently egregious to render it foreseeable that the withdrawal of the claimant from his post would cause him a psychiatric injury. It was not tantamount to dismissal, and he was told that if exonerated by the investigation, the FCO would try to find him another posting).

[Add note 364a to "reasonable" in line 7 on page [914]]

NOTE 364a. In the context of a decision to initiate disciplinary proceedings against an employee, the test is whether the decision was unreasonable in the sense that it was outside the range of reasonable decisions open to the employer: *Coventry University v Mian* [2014] E.L.R. 455, CA (it was not appropriate for the trial judge to make his own judgment of the merits of the allegation made against the claimant).

[Delete the text of n.372 from "Contrast" in line 10 to "decision" in line 13]   **11–89**

Running unnecessary risks

[Add to n.391]   **11–97**

In both *Dusek v Stormharbour Securities LLP* [2015] EWHC 722 (QB), and *Cassley v GMP Securities Europe LLP* [2015] EWHC 37 (QB), para.11-23a, above, the employers were held to owe a duty when procuring of chartered transportation services for their employees. Employers must ensure that the transportation providers are competent to perform the journey for which they are chartered in order that the employee is not exposed to unnecessary risk.

Duty regarding protection from crimes

[Add to text at the end of the paragraph]   **11–105**

The police do not owe a duty to make operational decisions in a way that protects officers taking part in time pressured operations from injuries due criminal activities, as this would impede their ability to act in the public interest.[418a]

NOTE 418a. *Rathband v Chief Constable of Northumbria* [2016] EWHC 181 (QB).

Employee placed with temporary employer

11–112 [*Note 441*]

Yates v National Trust reported at [2014] P.I.Q.R. P16.

LIABILITY FOR BREACH OF STATUTORY DUTY

2.—CATEGORIES OF BREACH OF STATUTORY DUTY

Careless performance of a statutory duty

[*Add to line 4 of n.23*]   **12–09**

. . . .[1999] P.N.L.R. 171.] In *CN v Poole BC* [2016] EWHC 569 claims on behalf of severely disabled children who alleged that a local authority negligently failed to exercise its protective powers under the Children Act 1989, were allowed to proceed, see Ch.2, para.2-331 above. [See Bailey and Bowman . . .

The common law duty of care

[*Note 36*]   **12–13**

Robinson v Chief Constable of West Yorkshire reported at [2014] P.I.Q.R. P14, CA.

[*Add to n.52*]   **12–18**

See also, *C v T BC* [2014] EWHC 2482 (QB) (no duty of care was owed by a local authority to a former employee for whom it had agreed to provide a reference in particular terms, to confine a response to police who requested information about the claimant when compiling an enhanced criminal record certificate, to the terms of the reference. There was no justification for imposing a duty of care on a supplier of information to the police which would discourage those who would in good faith provide assistance to the police on safeguarding issues [76 ff]).

3.—WHEN AN ACTION MAY BE BROUGHT

Illustrations: no intention to protect

[*Add to text after n.118*]   **12–34**

Health Regulations 1999.[118]] There was no private law duty on a primary healthcare trust to protect the claimant from foreseeable economic loss as a result of a breach of its obligations under reg.10 of the National Health Service (Performers Lists) Regulations 2004 SI No. 585.[118a] There was no parliamentary intention to protect a company alleging loss as a result of an error by the registrar of companies in discharging his duty under the Companies Act 2006 to record on the register those companies against whom a winding-up order had been made.[118b] [No private law action . . .

NOTE 118a. *Jowhari v NHS England* [2014] EWHC 4197 (QB), Sir Colin Mackay (the dentist alleged that his name had been unlawfully removed from the list of practitioners authorised to carry out NHS work; a claim in negligence also failed).

NOTE 118b. *Sebry v Companies House* [2015] EWHC 115 (QB), Ch.2, para.2-95, above (although no action lay for breach of statutory duty a common law duty of care was owed).

Further Illustrations: intention to protect

12–39   [*Replace text of n.147 after the reference to Watt v Fairfield Shipbuilding and Engineering Co Ltd*]

 . . . S.L.T. 1084, OH]. See also *McDonald v Department for Communities and Local Government* [2014] 3 WLR 1197, SC, approving the *Cherry Tree Machine* decision (reg.2(a) of the Asbestos Industry Regulations 1931 extended to factories and workshops where specified processes were carried on, it being the nature of the processes rather than the nature of the industry which were relevant; a lorry driver who made deliveries to a power station where lagging work required the mixing of asbestos powder with water was potentially within the ambit of the reg.). See article, *"Boost for asbestos claims"* N.L.J. 2014 (7628), 5.

Inadequacy of statutory remedy

12–55   [*Add to n.203*]

See also *Lillian Darby (Administratrix) v Richmond upon Thames LBC*, Ch.2, para.2-326, above.

4.—CIVIL LIABILITY AND HEALTH AND SAFETY REGULATIONS

The impact of section 69

12–70   [*Add to n.236*]

See generally Roy, "Without a safety net: litigating employers' liability claims after the Enterprise Act" 2015 J.P.I.L. (1), 15.

12–73   [*Delete the last sentence of n.240 including the reference to Kenedy v Cordia (Services) LLP*]

Avoiding the consequences of section 69

12–75   [*Add to n.247*]

 . . . UKHL 56]; also Limb and Cox "Section 69 of the Enterprise and Regulatory Reform Act 2013—plus ca change?" J.P.I. Law 2014, 1, 1.

6.—Defences to an Action for Breach of Statutory Duty

Momentary inattention or conscious acceptance of risk

[*Add to n.293*]   **12–89**

. . . para.6-87 et seq, above.] See also *Fulton v Vion Food Group Ltd* [2015] NICA 10 (where a safety glove worn by a butcher was cut by a knife he himself was using and shortly after he sustained an injury as a result of a further cut through the hole, the employer was found in breach of the Personal Protective Equipment at Work Regulations (Northern Ireland) 1993, but the sole cause of the accident was held to be the employee's own failure to alert his employer to the defect, notwithstanding a clear instruction for him to do so.

7.—Examples of Statutory Duty

(C) The Management of Health and Safety at Work Regulations 1999

Risk assessment

[*Add footnote reference 380a to "materialising" in line 15*]   **12–120**

Note 380a. See e.g. *Kennedy v Cordia (Services) LLP* [2016] 1 W.L.R. 597, SC (no sufficient risk assessment where there was a known risk of a home carer, employed by the defendant to visit patients in their homes, slipping on icy paths, but no consideration was given to individual protective measures other than an instruction, "of last resort," to wear appropriate footwear).

[*Add to line 9 of the text*]   **12–121**

. . . industrial disease.] The most logical way to approach a question as to the adequacy of the precautions taken by an employer is by considering the suitability and sufficiency of a risk assessment.[387a] [Even where a breach is proven . . .
Note 387a. *Per* Smith LJ in *Allison v London Underground Ltd* [2008] P.I.Q.R. P10, CA at [59], approved by the Supreme Court in *Kennedy v Cordia (Services) LLP* [2016] 1 W.L.R. 597, SC [89].

(D) The Workplace (Health, Safety and Welfare Regulations) 1992

The workplace

[*Add new footnote reference 445a to "is" in the last line*]   **12–139**

Note 445a. See e.g. *Coia v Portavardie Estates Ltd* 2015 Rep. L.R. 22, IH (where the defendant, an hotelier and lodge operator, provided its employee, the claimant, with a lodge, on the basis he should vacate it if a customer required it, the premises were not the claimant's workplace when, in the course of removing his personal possessions, he was injured by a loose pole in a cupboard).

CHAPTER 12

Floors and traffic routes

12–153   [*Add to the end of n.504*]

. . . the regulations]; appeal dismissed [2014] 3 WLR 1197, SC).

(E) The Work at Height Regulations 2005

Who is liable

12–177   [*Note 613*]

Yates v National Trust reported at [2014] P.I.Q.R. P16.

(G) The Provision and Use of Work Equipment Regulations 1998

Work equipment

12–206   [*Add to n.693*]

. . . 39, OH]; also *Coia v Portavardie Estates Ltd* 2015 Rep. L.R.22, IH, para.12–139, above (a loose pole in a cupboard, in a lodge provided to the claimant by his employer, which came away while he was moving his possessions, was not work equipment).

Use

12–208   [*Add footnote reference 694a to the sub heading*]

NOTE 694a. See e.g. *Rooney v Western Education and Library Board* [2015] NIQB 87 (the claimant, a canteen assistant at a school, suffered an laceration to her wrist when the handle of a mug she was drying broke: liability attached since the mug was an article provided by the employer for use in the workplace and the definition of "use' in Reg.2(1)(b) expressly included cleaning, of which drying was a part.

(J) The Personal Protective Equipment at Work Regulations 1992 (The Protective Equipment Regulations)

Introduction.

12–256   [*Add to line 2 of the text*]

. . . personal protective equipment where there is a risk to] an employee's [health or safety] while at work.[850a] [The presumption . . .
NOTE 850a. "At work" means "in the course of employment", so a home carer who travelled between the houses of her several clients was at work in the course of her journeys: *Kennedy v Cordia (Services) LLP* [2016] 1 W.L.R. 597, SC, at [100]. It is not the case that the risk to be protected against must arise from the work itself, as opposed, for instance, to the environment in which it is carried on: See [100] to [104].

[*Add to n.852*]

. . . into the matter.] See also *Kennedy v Cordia (Services) LLP* n. 850a, above (it was established that anti-slipping attachments were available at a modest cost; that they were used by other employers to address the risk of their employees slipping and falling on footpaths covered in snow and ice; that there was a body of research demonstrating that their use reduced the risk of slipping in wintry conditions; and there was expert evidence that such attachments made a difference).

[Add to text after n.866]   **12–258**

... worn them.[866]. Where an employee has been injured as a result of being exposed to a risk against which personal protective equipment should have been provided, and it is established the employee would have used it if provided, it will normally be reasonable to infer that the failure to provide the equipment made a material contribution to causation of an injury. Such an inference is reasonable because the equipment which the employer failed to provide would, by definition, have prevented the risk or rendered injury highly unlikely, so far as practicable.[866a]

NOTE 866a. *Kennedy v Cordia (Services) LLP* para.12-256, above, *per* Lords Reed and Hodge SCJs at [119]. They added that such an inference would not be appropriate if the cause of the accident was unconnected with the risk against which the employee should have been protected.

(K) The Manual Handling Operations Regulations 1992

The duty

[Add to text after n.910]   **12–268**

... bags of cement]; in a bus yard, the use of a mechanical gritter would have avoided the risk of injury inherent in spreading grit by hand, but the defendant failed to advance any defence that it was not reasonably practicable to avoid that particular manual handling operation.[910a] [An employer...

NOTE 910a. *King v RCO Support Services Ltd.*, n.891, above.

[Delete text to n.914]   **12–269**

[Add to text after n.913]

... manual handling operation]; where a learning support assistant injured her back in pushing a pupil in her wheelchair, but it was not reasonably practicable to avoid the use of manual wheelchairs and suitable risk assessments had been performed.[914]

NOTE 914. *Sloan v Rastrick High School Governors* [2015] P.I.Q.R. P1, CA.

[Add to text after n.925]   **12–276**

... reasonably practicable.[925] In contrast, where no satisfactory risk assessment had been performed, but an accident happened which was unconnected with any risk which the assessment would have identified or addressed, there was no liability. There was no causal connection between the breach of duty and the damage which in fact occurred.[925a]

NOTE 925a. *West Sussex CC v Fuller* [2015] EWCA Civ 189 (the claimant employee tripped on a staircase while she was delivering post around the office, no risk assessment had been carried out but she was not overloaded and the trip was the result of a simple misjudgement in placing her feet).

CHAPTER 13

DANGEROUS THINGS: RYLANDS V FLETCHER

1.—PRINCIPLES OF LIABILITY

(A) Introduction

The rule in Rylands v Fletcher

13–06   *[Add to n.13]*

See further *Northumbrian Water Ltd v Sir Robert McAlpine Ltd* [2014] EWCA Civ 685, Ch.9, para.9-72, above (no liability in nuisance, *Rylands* not being relied upon, for an escape of concrete into the claimant's sewer, in the course of building work carried out by the defendant).

3.—WATER

Liability for accumulating water.

13–58   *[Add to text after n.229]*

... will be liable.[229] As already noted,[229a] landowner is entitled to abstract subterranean water flowing in undefined channels beneath his land, regardless of the consequences to his neighbours.[229b]

NOTE 229a. See above, Ch.2 para.2-119.

NOTE 229b. *Chetwynd v Tunmore* [2016] EWHC 156 (QB) (no liability in negligence or nuisance where it was alleged that accumulating water in four lakes caused a significant decrease in the levels of lakes on adjoining land which were used as a commercial fishery; a claim under the Water Resources Act 1991, s.48A also failed, "but for" causation not being made out).

[84]

Water undertakers' liability for escapes from pipes

[*Add to n.302*]   **13–85**

In *Nicholson v Thames Water Utilities Ltd* [2014] EWHC 4249 (QB), a claim
for damage caused by an escape of sewage into domestic premises from the
main sewer, the water undertaker was not liable under s.209(1) since, *per*
Knowles J at [39]: "The language of subsection (1) makes plain the section
concerns an entity in its capacity as a water undertaker not as a sewerage
undertaker.

[*Add to the end of n.305*]

. . . New Roads and Street Works Act 1991.] As to liability under the 1991
Act see *Southern Gas Networks Plc v Thames Water Utilities Ltd* [2016]
EWHC 1669 (TCC) (payments made by a gas undertaker to its customers
after a water lek had damaged its apparatus were not recoverable under
s.82(1)(b) of the 1991 Act from the water company responsible for the leak
because the payments did not constitute "expenses reasonably incurred in
making good damage" within the meaning of the section. Nor could the
payments be recovered as damages for negligence: s.82 was part of a complete
code which precluded the recovery of damages for negligence.

Sewers and drains

[*Add to n.315*]   **13–90**

It should be noted that there is separate provision in the Water Industry Act
1991 for the duties and liabilities of water undertakers (for whom see
paras.13–84 ff above) and sewage undertakers. Thus in *Nicholson v Thames
Water Utilities Ltd* [2014] EWHC 4249 (QB), para.13–85, above, it was
pointed out that even if the defendant was both a water and sewage undertaker,
liability for an escape of sewage could not attach because the pipe from which
escape occurred was vested in the defendant qua water undertaker, not
otherwise.

CHAPTER 15

PRODUCT LIABILITY

2.—GENERAL PRINCIPLES OF LIABILITY

(A) Under the Consumer Protection Act 1987: Part 1 "Product Liability"

Expectation of Consumers

15–20 [*Add to text after n.68*]

The claimant need not specify with precision or accuracy the exact way that the product is defective, but instead that it had fallen below the level of safety which could be generally expected of the product.[68a]
NOTE 68a. *Hufford v Samsung Electronics (UK) Ltd* [2014] EWHC 2956 (TCC).

Defect and Causation

15–30 [*Add to n.102 after the case reference in line 1*]

. . . P13, CA]; also *Love v Halfords Ltd* [2014] P.I.Q.R. P20. [See further . . .

[*Add to text at end of paragraph*]

The claimant cannot recover for damage to property in circumstances where expert evidence suggests that fire which caused the damage originates outside of the product.[102a]
NOTE 102a. *Hufford v Samsung Electronics (UK) Ltd* [2014] EWHC 2956 (TCC), para.15-20, above.

Damage

15–33 [*Add footnote 106a to "use" in line 5*]

NOTE 106a. The use of a golf clubhouse damaged by fire was not private simply because the club was owned by the members of the club; and given the size of the membership and the range of commercial activities carried on there it could not properly be said to be ordinarily intended for private use and occupation: *Renfrew Golf Club v Motocaddy Ltd* [2015] CSOH 173.

3.—LIABILITY IN CONTRACT

Strict Liability

[Add new n.174a to "included" in the last line]   **15–53**

NOTE 174a. From 1st October 2015 Ch.2 of Pt.1 of the Consumer Rights Act 2015 implies terms into a contract by which a trader is to supply goods to a consumer. A consumer is defined in s.2(3) as "an individual acting for purposes that are wholly or mainly outside that individual's trade, business, craft or profession"; and a trader is defined in s.2(2) as "a person acting for purposes relating to that person's trade, business, craft or profession, whether acting personally or through another person acting in the trader's name or on the trader's behalf." In such contracts the Sale of Goods Act 1979 will no longer be the source of the traders' obligation to supply goods of satisfactory quality and which are fit for purpose. These will be implied into consumer contracts by ss.9 and 10 of the Consumer Rights Act. The Sale of Goods Act 1979 will continue to be the source of implied obligations in contracts between traders. See further Appendix A to this Supplement which sets out the principal effect of the Act so far as it lies within the scope of this work.

Defences

[Add to text at the end of the paragraph]   **15–86**

 . . . before use.] Any term in a consumer contract or a consumer notice which purports to exclude or restrict liability for death or personal injury resulting from negligence will not be effective.[284a] A term in a consumer contract or a consumer notice which purports to exclude or restrict liability in negligence other than for death or personal injury is subject to a test of fairness.[284b]

NOTE 284a. s.65(1) of the Consumer Rights Act 2015 which came into force on 1st October 2015.

NOTE 284b. s.62 of the Consumer Rights Act 2015. See further Ch.2, para.2-214, Ch.4, para.4-85 Ch.8, paras. 8-43, 8-45 and Appendix A to this Supplement.

CHAPTER 16

DEATH AND CAUSES OF ACTION

1.—THE COMMON LAW

The rules at common law

16–02   [*Note 11*]

Haxton v Philips Electronics UK Ltd reported at [2014] P.I.Q.R. P11, CA.

2.—THE ACCRUAL OF A CAUSE OF ACTION

(A) The Fatal Accidents Act 1976

The measure of damages

16–27   [*Delete the second sentence of n.101 and replace as follows*]

. . . .16–64, below]. The multiplier to be applied in a fatal accidents claim, when assessing the number of years for the claimant's dependency, is to be selected as at the date of trial: *Knauer v Ministry of Justice* [2016] UKSC 9, [2016] 2 W.L.R. 672, SC overruling *Cookson v Knowles* [1979] AC 556 and *Graham v Dodds* [1983] 1 WLR 808. [In *White v Esab Group (UK) Ltd* . . .

16–28a   [*Add new paragraph to text*]

There is no jurisdiction to award damages for loss of intangible benefits. Where the consequences of the loss of a spouse can be valued in financial terms they can be the subject of a claim, but where they cannot be so valued then they fall to be compensated through the mechanism of bereavement damages. Therefore, a wife could not recover damages representing the "additional value and convenience" of her deceased husband performing tasks, when compared to having the same tasks performed by a third party contractor.[107a] The costs of the lost services were reflected in the damages awarded, but the intangible benefits were not.

NOTE 107a. *Mosson v Spousal (London) Ltd* [2016] 4 W.L.R. 28.

No presumption of pecuniary loss

16–41   [*Add to n.135*]

See e.g. n.138a, below.

Where marriage has been annulled or dissolved or parties are judicially separated

[Add to text at the end of the paragraph]   **16–42**

... can be taken into account.] Where it was accepted that the claimant, the former wife of the deceased, had been on the point of reconciliation with him, dependency was assessed on the basis of an 80% chance that a reconciliation would have been permanent.[138a]

NOTE 138a. *Hayes v South East Coast Ambulance Service NHS Foundation Trust* [2015] EWHC 18 (QB).

Other considerations in ascertaining pecuniary loss

[Note 144]   **16–43**

Haxton v Philips Electronics UK Ltd reported at [2014] P.I.Q.R. P11, CA.

The multiplier

[Add full stop immediately before n.211 and delete the text thereafter   **16–63**
including footnotes 212 to 216]

[Add new text after n.211]

In *Knauer v Ministry of Justice*[212] the Supreme Court endorsed the approach in the Ogden Tables, departing from earlier decisions[213] which required the multiplier to be calculated from the date of death. The dicta of Lord Lloyd in *Wells v Wells*[214] were approved as applying equally to fatal and non-fatal accident cases.

NOTE 212. [2016] 2 W.L.R. 672, SC.

NOTE 213. *Cookson v Knowles* [1976] A.C. 556, *Graham v Dodds* [1983] 1 W.L.R. 808, HL and *White v Esab Group (UK) Ltd* [2002] P.I.Q.R. Q 6.

NOTE 214. Above n.209.

CHAPTER 17

INSURANCE AND OTHER COMPENSATION SCHEMES

1.—COMPULSORY INSURANCE

(A) Motor Insurance

Motor Insurance

17–03 [*Add to n.6*]

... April 3, 2000.] In *Vnuk v Zavarovalnica Triglav dd* (C-162/13) [2016] RTR 10, the ECJ decided that the compulsory third party motor insurance requirement under art.3 of Directive 72/166 was applicable to the use of a tractor on a private farm yard. See further Bevan, "Ignore at your peril" N.L.J. 2014, (7628), 7. In *UK Insurance Ltd v Holden* [2016] EWHC 264 (QB); [2016] 4 W.L.R. 38; the Court of Appeal, obiter, found that limiting compulsory insurance to roads and public places was incompatible with Directive 72/166 as interpreted in *Vnuk*. See Holden, "Vnuk: An involuntary risk transfer" S.J. 2016, 160(11), 20; Bevan, "Still driving dangerously" N.L.J. 2016, 166(7693), 18, and (same author) "Tinkering at the edges" J.P.I. Law 2015, 3, 138.

Foreign Accidents.

17–14 [*Add to n.40*]

... EWCA Civ 1543]; *Moreno v M.I.B.* [2015] Lloyd's Rep. I.R. 535. The M.I.B. remains liable to compensate the injured party (subject to the insured's liability) even where the foreign insurer of the vehicle involved has had its licence revoked and entered insolvency before a claim is presented: *Wigley-Foster v Wilson, The Times*, July 5, 2016, CA.

Exceptions in English and Welsh cases

17–15 [*Add to n.47*]

... sell the drugs illegally.] However in *Delaney v Secretary of State for Transport* [2015] EWCA Civ 172 it was held in the Court of Appeal that cl.6.1(e)(iii) of the Uninsured Drivers' Agreement was itself in breach of the UK's obligations under European Directives, namely Directive 72/166, Directive 84/5 and Directive 90/232. The decision of the trial judge that the breach was sufficiently serious to entitle the claimant to *Francovich* damages (cf Ch.4, para.4-244, above) was upheld. Further, it was held in *Smith v Stratton* [2015] EWCA Civ 1413 that *Francovich* damages were the only remedy available to a claimant who fell within clause 6 of the Uninsured Drivers Agreement. Non-compatibility with EU law did not enable the Court to read the agreement in a different way.

3.—Criminal Injuries Compensation

The new scheme

[*Add to n.101*]   **17–32**

See *RS v Criminal Injuries Compensation Authority* [2014] 1 W.L.R. 1313, CA, in which it was said that caution should be exercised in drawing assistance from common law cases when considering the words "immediate aftermath", see Ch.2, para.2-152 above.

Crime of violence

[*Note 103*]   **17–33**

CICA v First-Tier Tribunal (Social Entitlement Chamber) reported at [2014] P.I.Q.R. P10, CA.

[*Add new footnote reference 103a to "foetus" in sub paragraph 4(1)(e)*]

Note 103a. Under an earlier Scheme a mother's excessive consumption of alcohol, causing her child to be born with permanent damage from foetal alcohol spectrum disorder, did not entitle the child to compensation, since the child had no separate legal personality when the damage occurred: *CP v Criminal Injuries Compensation Authority* [2015] 2 W.L.R. 463, CA.

[*Note 105*]   **17–34**

CICA v First-Tier Tribunal (Social Entitlement Chamber) reported at [2014] P.I.Q.R. P10, CA.

Procedure for making applications

[*Add new footnote reference 124a to "applications" in the heading*]   **17–41**

Note 124a. Victims of criminal injury who lack capacity should make any application to the CICA by an attorney acting under a registered enduring power of attorney or lasting power of attorney for property and financial affairs, or some other person authorised by the Court of Protection to make the application: see *Newcastle City Council v PV* [2015] EWCOP 22, Senior Master Lush, in which various aspects of the functions of the CoP and the CICA in relation to such applications are discussed.

[*Add to n.126*]

See *Colefax v First Tier Tribunal (Social Entitlement Chamber)* [2014] P.I.Q.R. P21, CA (the CICA was entitled not to waive the two year time limit where, although a link between an applicant's epilepsy and an assault upon him was only diagnosed after two years, he had suffered other serious injuries in the incident and an application could and should have been made earlier. It was said that while paras. 53, 56 and 57 of the scheme made some provision for satisfying claims in respect of late manifested or diagnosed injuries by reappraisal, they did not assist a victim where a serious injury manifested itself, or was first diagnosed as caused by an incident, more than two years after, where an application for compensation had not already been brought on time. Compensation for such an applicant had to rest on satisfying the conditions imposed by paras.18 (a) and (b) and even then, the waiver of the time limit was a matter of discretion for the authority).

LEGISLATIVE NOTE—THE CONSUMER RIGHTS ACT 2015

The Consumer Rights Act 2015

The Consumer Rights Act 2015 came into force on 1st October 2015. Despite **A–1** being predominantly a statute that deals with consumer contracts[1] the Act has important implications for some of the subjects covered in this book. In particular, the Act provides the source of the implied term of reasonable care in consumer contracts for services; governs unfair terms in consumer contracts (with the Unfair Contract Terms Act 1977 continuing to apply to contracts between businesses); and provides the source of the obligations of satisfactory quality and fitness for purpose in consumer contracts, which may be important in defective products cases. This legislative note is intended to provide guidance on these areas. However, the 2015 Act also contains numerous provisions regarding proof and remedies that go beyond the scope of this work.

NOTE 1. See paragraph A-2 below.

Meaning of Consumer

A consumer is defined in s.2(3) of the Consumer Rights Act as "an individual **A–2** acting for purposes that are wholly or mainly outside that individual's trade, business, craft or profession.

Meaning of Trader

A trader is defined in s.2(2) as "a person acting for purposes relating to that **A–3** person's trade, business, craft or profession, whether acting personally or through another person acting in the trader's name or on the trader's behalf."

Contracts for Sale of Goods

The Consumer Rights Act 2015 implies terms into a contract between a **A–4** consumer and trader for the sale or supply of goods. Practitioners dealing with liability for defective products acquired after 1st October 2015 must consider whether the Consumer Rights Act governs the transaction. The terms implied by the Sales of Goods Act 1979 continue to apply to contracts other than those between a consumer and a trader.

The contractual obligations in relation to quality and fitness in contracts **A–5** between traders and consumers, are provided by Consumer Rights Act 2015 s.9. This provides that "every contract to supply goods is to be treated as including a term that the quality of the goods is satisfactory."

Goods will be satisfactory if they meet the standard that a reasonable **A–6** consumer would consider satisfactory.[2] This implied term does not extend to matters specifically drawn to the attention of the consumer prior to the making of the contract, or matters which an examination undertaken by the consumer prior to the entry into the contract ought to reveal or matters which would have been revealed by a reasonable examination of a sample relied upon by the consumer in purchasing the goods.[3]

NOTE 2. Consumer Rights Act 2015 s.9(2).

NOTE 3. See s.9(4).

A–7 Section 10 of the Act provides that if in a contract to supply goods a consumer, before the contract is made, "makes known to the trader (expressly or by implication) any particular purpose for which the consumer is contracting for the goods" then "the contract is to be treated as including a term that the goods are reasonably fit for that purpose, whether or not that is a purpose for which goods of that kind are usually supplied."[4] The term is not implied where "the circumstances show that the consumer does not rely, or it is unreasonable for the consumer to rely, on the skill or judgment of the trader."[5] The section is not limited to goods order for a specific purpose. Where the product purchased has a usual purpose a term is implied that the product will be fit to fulfil that purpose.[6]

NOTE 4. Consumer Rights Act 2015 s.10(3).

NOTE 5. s.10(4).

NOTE 6. See *Priest v Last* [1903] 2 KB 148.

Contract for Services

A–8 A contract between a consumer and a trader for the provision of services will contain an implied term that "the trader must perform the service with reasonable care and skill."[9] In any case concerning the negligent provision of services by a trader to a consumer where the contract was entered into after 1st October 2015 this provision will be the source of the contractual obligation concurrent to the tortious duty of care. The Supply of Goods and Services Act 1982 s.13 will continue to apply to contracts other than those between a consumer and a trader.

NOTE 9. s.49(1).

Unfair Terms

A–9 Exclusions or limitations of liability contained in "consumer contracts" and "consumer notices" will be subject to control under Pt. 2 of the Consumer Rights Act 2015. A consumer contract is defined in s.61 as a "contract between a trader and a consumer" not including a "contract of employment or apprenticeship." A consumer notice is defined in s.61 as "an announcement, whether or not in writing, and any other communication or purported communication" where it is "reasonable to assume it is intended to be seen or heard by a consumer" which "relates to rights or obligations as between a trader and a consumer" or "purports to exclude or restrict a trader's liability to a consumer." Exclusions or limitations of liability in all other contracts or notice continue to be governed by the Unfair Contract Terms Act 1977.

A–10 Any term in a consumer contract or a consumer notice which purports to exclude or restrict liability for death or personal injury resulting from negligence will not be effective.[10] Personal injury "any disease and any impairment of physical or mental condition."[11] Negligence is defined as breach of an "obligation to take reasonable care or exercise reasonable skill in the performance of a contract where the obligation arises from an express or implied term of the contract," a "common law duty to take reasonable care or exercise reasonable skill" or "the common duty of care imposed by the Occupiers' Liability Act 1957."[12] Further, agreement to such a term will not be effective, without more, to substantiate a defence of voluntary acceptance of the risk.[13]

NOTE 10. Consumer Rights Act 2015 s.65(1).
NOTE 11. Consumer Rights act 2015 s.65(3).
NOTE 12. Consumer Rights Act 2015 s.65(4).
NOTE 13. Consumer Rights Act 2015 s.65(2).

A term in a consumer contract or a consumer notice which purports to exclude **A–11** or restrict liability in negligence other than for death or personal injury will be subject to a test of fairness. An unfair term or unfair notice will not be binding on the consumer. The test of unfairness of a consumer contract term is set out in Consumer Rights Act 2015 s.62(4). This provides that a term will be unfair "if, contrary to the requirement of good faith, it causes a significant imbalance in the parties' rights and obligations under the contract to the detriment of the consumer." When making this judgement the court must take into account "the subject matter of the contract" and "all the circumstances existing when the term was agreed and to all of the other terms of the contract or of any other contract on which it depends."[14] The test of unfairness of a consumer notice is set out in Consumer Rights Act 2015 s.62(6). This provides that a consumer notice will be unfair "if, contrary to the requirement of good faith, it causes a significant imbalance in the parties' rights and obligations under the contract to the detriment of the consumer." When making this judgement the court must take into account "the subject matter of the notice" and "all the circumstances existing when the rights or obligations to which it relates arose and to the terms of any contract on which it depends."[15]

NOTE 14. s.62(5)
NOTE 15. s.62(7)

The Supreme Court considered the operation of this test in *Cavendish Square* **A–12** *Holdings BV v Makdassi*.[16] They approved the guidance given by the European Court of Justice in *Aziz v Caxia d'Estalvis de Catalunya, Tarragona I Manresa*.[17] In deciding whether a term or notice is fair the court must ask whether it places the consumer in a significantly worse position than they would be under national law ("significant imbalance") and whether the consumer would have agreed to the term in individual contract negotiations, including giving consideration to whether the term or notice goes beyond what is necessary to secure the objective pursued by the term or notice ("contrary to the requirements of good faith"). This test may be wider than the familiar test of reasonableness found in the Unfair Contract Terms Act 1977.

NOTE 16. [2015] UKSC 67; [2015] 3 W.L.R. 1373.
NOTE 17. [2013] 3 CMLR 89.